THE

JESUS OF HISTORY

THE JESUS OF HISTORY

T. R. GLOVER

GYAN

Published by

Gyan Publishing House
5, Ansari Road
Daryaganj, New Delhi-110002
Phone: 011-47034999, 9811692060
E-mail: books@gyanbooks.com

Distribution Network
gyanbooks.com
India, USA, Canada, UK, Australia, France

ISBN : 978-81-212-9745-5 (PB)
First Published, 1917

2nd Impression 2023

Printed at: Gyan Press, Delhi.

THE JESUS OF HISTORY
Author: T. R. GLOVER

THE JESUS OF HISTORY

BY

T. R. GLOVER

FELLOW OF ST. JOHN'S COLLEGE, CAMBRIDGE
UNIVERSITY LECTURER IN ANCIENT HISTORY

WITH A FOREWORD

BY

THE ARCHBISHOP OF CANTERBURY

1917

TO

RICHARD GLOVER

FOREWORD

I REGARD it as a high privilege to be associated with this volume. Many who know and value Mr. Glover's work on *The Conflict of Religions in the Early Roman Empire* must have wistfully desired to secure from his graphic pen just such a book as is here given to the world. He possesses the rare power of reverently handling familiar truths or facts in such manner as to make them seem to be almost new. There are few gifts more precious than this at a time when our familiarity with the greatest and most sacred of all narratives is a chief hindrance to our ready appreciation of its living power. I believe that no one will read Mr. Glover's chapters, and especially his description of the parable-teaching given by our Lord, without a sense of having been introduced to a whole series of fresh and fruitful thoughts. He has expanded for us with the force, the clearness, and the power of vivid illustration which we have learned to expect from him, the meaning of a sentence in the earlier volume I have alluded to, where he insists that, "Jesus of Nazareth does stand in the center of human history, that He has brought God and man into a new relation, that He is the present concern of every one of us and that there is more in Him than we have yet accounted for."[1]

In accordance with its title, the single theme of the

[1] *The Conflict of Religions in the Early Roman Empire*, p. 157

book is "The Jesus of History," but the student or exponent of dogmatic theology will find abundant material in its pages.

I commend it confidently, both to single students and to those who nowadays, in happily increasing numbers, meet together for common study; and I congratulate those who belong to the Student Christian Movement upon this notable addition to the books published in connection with their far-reaching work.

RANDALL CANTUAR.

LAMBETH,
Advent Sunday, 1916.

PREFACE

This book has grown out of lectures upon the historical Jesus given in a good many cities of India during the winter of 1915–16. Recast and developed, the lectures were taken down in shorthand in Calcutta; they were revised in Madras; and most of them were wholly rewritten, where and when in six following months leisure was available, in places so far apart as Colombo, Maymyo, Rangoon, Kodaikanal, Simla, and Poona. The reader will not expect a heavy apparatus of references to books which were generally out of reach.

Here and there are incorporated passages (rehandled) from articles that have appeared in *The Conservative Quarterly*, *The Nation*, *The Expositor*, and elsewhere.

Those who themselves have tried to draw the likeness attempted in this book will best understand, and perhaps most readily forgive, failures and mistakes, or even worse, in my drawing. The aim of the book, as of the lectures, is, after all, not to achieve a final presentment of the historical Jesus, but to suggest lines of study that will deepen our interest in him and our love of him.

T. R. G.

Poona, *August*, 1916

PUBLISHERS' NOTE

"The Jesus of History" was prepared for the British Student Christian Movement, and published in Great Britain by that organization. The author is so well-known in this country, especially among students, that it has seemed to the publishers that his suggestive book should be made available in America.

CONTENTS

CHAPTER I

THE STUDY OF THE GOSPELS

CHAPTER II

CHILDHOOD AND YOUTH

CHAPTER III

THE MAN AND HIS MIND

CHAPTER IV

THE TEACHER AND THE DISCIPLES

THE BACKGROUND

CHAPTER VI

JESUS AND MAN

CHAPTER VII

JESUS' TEACHING UPON SIN

CHAPTER VIII

THE CHOICE OF THE CROSS

CHAPTER IX

THE CHRISTIAN CHURCH IN THE ROMAN EMPIRE

That one Face, far from vanish, rather grows,
Or decomposes but to recompose,
Become my universe that feels and knows.

ROBERT BROWNING
Epilogue *to Dramatis Personæ*

THE JESUS OF HISTORY

CHAPTER I

THE STUDY OF THE GOSPELS

If one thing more than another marks modern thought, it is a new insistence on fact. In every sphere of study there is a growing emphasis on verification. Where a generation ago a case seemed to be closed, to-day in the light of new facts it is reopened. Matters that to our grandfathers were trivialities, to be summarily dismissed, are seriously studied. Again and again we find the most fruitful avenues opened to us by questions that another age might have laughed out of a hearing; to-day they suggest investigation of facts insufficiently known, and of the difficult connections between them. In psychology and in medicine the results of this new tendency are evident in all sorts of ways—new methods in the treatment of the sick, new inquiries as to the origin of diseases and the possibilities of their prevention, attempts to get at the relations between the soul and body, and a very new open-mindedness as to the spiritual nature and its working and experiences. In other fields of learning it is the same.

To the modern student of man and his history the old easy way of excluding religion as an absurdity, the light prediction of its speedy, or at least its eventual, disappearance from the field of human life, and other dogmatisms of the like kind, are almost unintelligible. We realize that religion in some form is a natural working of the human spirit, and, whatever place we give to religion in the conduct of our own lives, as students of history we reckon with the religious instinct as a factor of the highest import, and we give to religious systems and organizations—above all, to religious teachers and leaders—a more sympathetic and a profounder study. Carlyle's lecture on Mohammed, in his course on "Heroes and Hero Worship," may be taken as a landmark for English people in this new treatment of history.

The Christian Church, whether we like it or not, has been a force of unparalleled power in human affairs; and prophecies that it will no longer be so, and allegations that by now it has ceased to be so, are not much made by cautious thinkers. There is evidence that the influence of the Christian Church, so far from ebbing, is rising—evidence more obvious when we reflect that the influence of such a movement is not to be quickly guessed from the number of its actual adherents. A century and a quarter of Christian missions in India have resulted in so many converts—a million and a quarter is no slight outcome; but that is a small part of the story. All over India the old religious systems are being subjected to a new study by their own adherents; their weak points are being felt; there are reform movements, new apologetics, compromises, defenses—all sorts of indications of ferment and transition. There can be little question that while many things go to the making of an age, the prime impulse to all this intellectual, religious, and moral upheaval was the faith of Christian missionaries that Jesus Christ would bring about what we actually see. They believed—and they were laughed at for their belief—that Jesus Christ was still a real power, permanent and destined to hold a larger place in the affairs of men; and we see that they were right. Jesus remains the very heart and soul of the Christian movement, still controlling men, still capturing men—against their wills very often—changing men's lives and using them for ends they never dreamed of. So much is plain to the candid observer, whatever the explanation.

We find, further, another fact of even more significance to the historian who will treat human experience with seriousness and sympathy. The cynical view that delusion and error in a real world have peculiar power in human affairs, may be dismissed; no serious student of history could hold it. For those who believe, as we all do at heart, that the world is rational, that real effects follow real causes, and conversely that behind great movements lie great forces, the fact must weigh enormously that wherever the Christian Church, or a section of it, or a single Christian, has put upon Jesus Christ a higher emphasis—above all where everything has been centered in Jesus Christ—there has been an increase of power for Church, or community, or man. Where new value has been found in Jesus Christ, the Church has risen in power, in energy, in appeal, in victory. Paul of Tarsus progressively found more in Christ, expected more of him, trusted him more; and his faith was justified. If Paul was wrong, how did he capture the Christian Church for his ideas? If he was wrong, how is it that when Luther caught his meaning, reinterpreted him and laid the same emphasis on Jesus Christ with his *Nos nihil sumus, Christus solus est omnia*,[1] once more the hearts of men were won by the higher doctrine of Christ's person and power, and a new era followed the new emphasis? How is it that, when John Wesley made the same discovery, and once more staked all on faith in Christ, again the Church felt the pulse of new life? On the other hand, where through a nebulous philosophy men have minimized Jesus, or where, through some weakness of the human mind, they have sought the aid of others and relegated Jesus Christ to a more distant, even if a higher, sphere—where, in short, Christ is not the living center of everything, the value of the Church has declined, its life has waned. That, to my own mind, is the most striking and outstanding fact in history. There must be a real explanation of a thing so signal in a rational universe.

The explanation in most human affairs comes after the recognition of the fact. There our great fact stands of the significance of Jesus Christ—a more wonderful thing as we study it more. We may fail to explain it, but we must recognize it. One of the weaknesses of the Church to-day is—put bluntly—that Christians are not making enough of Jesus Christ.

We find again that, where Jesus Christ is most real, and means most, there we are apt to see the human mind reach a fuller freedom and achieve more. There is a higher civilization, a greater emphasis on the value of human life and character, and a stronger endeavor for the utmost development of all human material,

[1] "We are nothing; Christ alone is all."

if we may so call the souls and faculties of men. Why should there be this correspondence between Jesus of Nazareth and human life? It is best brought out, when we realize what he has made of Christian society, and contrast it with what the various religions have left or produced in other regions—the atrophy of human nature.

In fine, there is no figure in human history that signifies more. Men may love him or hate him, but they do it intensely. If he was only what some say, he ought to be a mere figure of antiquity by now. But he is more than that; Jesus is not a dead issue; he has to be reckoned with still; and men, who are to treat mankind seriously, must make the intellectual effort to understand the man on whom has been centered more of the interest and the passion of the most serious and the best of mankind than on any other. The real secret is that human nature is deeply and intensely spiritual, and that Jesus satisfies it at its most spiritual point.

The object before us in these pages is the attempt to know Jesus, if we can, in a more intimate and intelligent way than we have done—at least, to put before our minds the great problem, Who is this Jesus Christ? and to try to answer it.

One answer to this question is that Jesus was nothing, never was anything, but a myth developed for religious purposes; that he never lived at all. This view reappears from time to time, but so far it has not appealed to any who take a serious interest in history. No historian of the least repute has committed himself to the theory. Desperate attempts have been made to discredit the Christian writers of the first two centuries; it has been emphasized that Jesus is not mentioned in secular writers of the period, and the passage in Tacitus (*Annals*, xv. 44) has been explained away as a Christian interpolation, or, more gaily, by reviving the wild notion that Poggio Bracciolini forged the whole of the *Annals*. But such trifling with history and literature does not serve. No scholar accepts the theory about Poggio—and yet if the passage about Christ is to be got rid of, this is the better way of the two; for there is nothing to countenance the view that the chapter is interpolated, or to explain when or by whom it was done—the wish is father to the thought. Christians are twice mentioned by Suetonius in dealing with Emperors of the first century, though in one passage the reading *Chrestus* for *Christus* has suggested to some scholars that another man is meant; the confusion was a natural one and is instanced elsewhere, but we need not press the matter. The argument from silence is generally recognized as an uncertain one. Sir James Melville, living at the Court of Mary, Queen of Scots, does not, I learn, mention John Knox—"whom he could not have failed to mention if Knox had really existed and played the part assigned to him by his partisans," and so forth. It might be as possible and as reasonable to prove that the Brahmo Samaj never existed, by demonstrating four hundred years hence—or two thousand—that it is not mentioned in *In Memoriam*, nor in *The Ring and the Book*, nor in George Meredith's novels, nor (more strangely) in any of Mr. Kipling's surviving works, which definitely deal with India. None of these writers, it may be replied, had any concern to mention the Brahmo Samaj. And when one surveys the Greek and Roman writers of the first century A. D., which of them had any concern to refer to Jesus and his disciples, beyond the historians who do? Indeed, the difficulty is to understand why some of these men should have written at all; harder still, why others should have wanted to read their poems and orations and commonplace books. One argument, advanced in India a few years ago, against the historical value of the Gospels may be revived by way of illustration. Would not Virgil and Horace, it was asked, have taken notice of the massacre at Bethlehem, if it was historical? Would they not? it was replied, when they both had died years before its traditional date.

But the distinction between Christian and secular writers is not one that will weigh much with a serious historian. Until we have reason to distinguish between book and book, the evidence must be treated on exactly the same principles. To say abruptly that, because Luke was a Christian and Suetonius a pagan, Luke is not worthy of the credence given to Suetonius, is a line of approach that will most commend itself to those who have read neither author. To gain a real knowledge of historical truth, the historian's methods must be slower and more cautious, he must know his author intimately—his habits of mind, his turns of style, his preferences, his gifts for seeing the real issue—and always the background, and the ways of thinking that prevail in the background. An ancient writer is not necessarily negligible because he records, and perhaps believes, miracles or marvels or omens which a modern would never notice. It is bad criticism that has made a popular legend of the unreliable character of Herodotus. As our knowledge of antiquity grows, and we become able to correct our early impressions, the credit of Herodotus rises steadily, and to-day those who study him most closely have the highest opinion of him.

We may, then, without prejudice, take the evidence of Paul of Tarsus on the historicity of Jesus, and examine it. If we are challenged as to the genuineness of Paul's epistles, let us tell our questioner to read them. Novels have been written in the form of correspondence; but Paul's letters do not tell us all that a novelist or a forger would—there are endless gaps, needless references to unknown persons (needless to us, or to anybody apart from the people themselves), constant occupation with questions which we can only dimly discover from Paul's answers. The letters are genuine letters—written for the occasion to particular people, and not meant for us. The stamp of genuineness is on them—of life, real life. The German scholar, Norden, in his *Kunstprosa*, says there is much in Paul that he does not understand, but he catches in him again after three hundred years that note of life that marks the great literature of Greece. That is not easily forged. Luther and Erasmus were right when they said—each of them has said it, however it happened—that Paul "spoke pure flame." The letters, and the theology and its influence, establish at once Paul's claim to be a historical character. We may then ask, how a man of his ability failed to observe that a non-historical Jesus, a pure figment, was being palmed off on him—on a contemporary, it should be marked—and by a combination of Jesus' own disciples with earlier friends of Paul, who were trying to exterminate them. Paul knew priests and Pharisees; he knew James and John and Peter; and he never detected that they were in collusion, yes, and to the point of martyring Stephen

—to impose on him and on the world a non-historical Jesus. To such straits are we brought, if Jesus never existed. History becomes pure nonsense, and knowledge of historical fact impossible; and, it may be noted, all knowledge is abolished if history is beyond reach.

But we are not dependent on books for our evidence of the historicity of Jesus. The whole story of the Church implies him. He is inwrought in every feature of its being. Every great religious movement, of which we know, has depended on a personal impulse, and has behind it some real, living and inspiring personality. It is true that at a comparatively late stage of Hinduism a personal devotion to Shri Krishna grew up, just as in the hour of decline of the old Mediterranean paganism we find Julian the Apostate using a devotional language to Athena at Athens that would have astonished the contemporaries of Pericles. But Jesus, Buddha, and Mohammed stand on a very different footing from Krishna and Athena, even if we concede the view of some scholars that Krishna was once a man, and the contention of Euhemerus, a pre-Christian Greek, that all the gods had once been human. If we posit that Jesus did not exist, we shall be involved in other difficulties as to the story of the Church. Mr. F. C. Conybeare, an Oxford scholar avowedly not in allegiance to the Christian Church, has characterized some of the reconstructions made by contemporary anti-Christian writers as more miraculous than the history they are trying to correct.

We come now to the Gospels; and in what follows, and throughout the book, we shall confine ourselves to the first three Gospels. Great as has been, and must be, the influence of the Fourth Gospel, in the present stage of historical criticism it will serve our purpose best to postpone the use of a source which we do not fully understand. The exact relations of history and interpretation in the Fourth Gospel—the methods and historical outlook of the writer—cannot yet be said to be determined. "Only those who have merely trifled with the problems it suggests are likely to speak dogmatically upon the subject."[1] This is not to abandon the Fourth Gospel; for it is a document which we could not do without in early Church History, and which has vindicated its place in the devotional life in every Christian generation. But, for the present, the first Three Gospels will be our chief sources.

The Gospels have, of course, been attacked again and again. Sober criticism has raised the question as to whether here and there traces may be found of the touch of a later hand—for example, were there two asses or one, when Jesus rode into Jerusalem? has the baptismal formula at the end of Matthew been adjusted to the creed of Nicæa? In the following pages the attempt will be made to base what is said not on isolated texts, which may—and of course may not—have been touched, but on the general tenor of the books. A single episode or phrase may suffer change from a copyist's hand, from inadvertence or from theological predilection. The character of the Personality set forth in the Gospels is less susceptible of alteration.

This point is at once of importance, for the suggestion has been made that we cannot be sure of any par-

---

[1] Canon Streeter in *Foundations*, p. 82.

ticular statement, episode, incident or saying in the Gospels—taken by itself. Let us for the moment imagine a more sweeping theory still—that no single episode or incident or saying of Jesus in the Gospels is authentic at all. What follows? The great historian, E. A. Freeman of Oxford, once said that a false anecdote may be good history; it may be sound evidence for character, for, to obtain currency, a false anecdote has also to be true; it must be, in our proverbial phrase, "if not true, well invented." Even if exaggeration and humor contribute to give it a twist, the essence of parody is that it parodies—it must conform to the original even where it leaves it. A good story-teller will hardly tell the same story of Mr. Roosevelt and the Archbishop of Canterbury—unless it happens to be true, and then he will be cautious. "Truth," to quote another proverb, "is stranger than fiction"; because fiction has to go warily to be probable, and must be, more or less, conventional. The story a man invents about another has to be true in some recognizable way to character—as a little experiment in this direction will show. The inventor of a story must have the gift of the caricaturist and of the bestower of nicknames; he must have a shrewd eye for the real features of his victim. Jesus, then, was a historical person; and about him we have a mass of stories in the Gospels, which our theory for the moment asks us to say are all false; but they have a certain unity of tone, and they agree in pointing to a character of a certain type, and the general aspects and broad outlines of that character they make abundantly clear. Even on such a hypothesis we can know something of the character of Jesus. But the hypothesis is gratuitous, and absurd, as the paragraphs that follow may help to show. The Gospels are essentially true and reliable records of a historical person.

A survey of some of the outstanding features of the Gospels should do something to assure their reader of their historical value. But there is a necessary caution to be given at this moment. When Aristotle discusses happiness, he adds a curious limitation—"as the man of sense would define." He postulates a certain intelligence of the matter in hand. Similarly Longinus, the greatest of ancient critics, says that in literature sure judgment is the outcome of long experience. In matters of historical and literary criticism, a certain instinct is needed, conscious or unconscious, perhaps more often the latter, which without a serious interest and a long experience no man is likely to have.

The Gospels are not properly biographies; they consist of collections of reminiscences—memories and fragments that have survived for years, and sometimes the fragment is little more than a phrase. Such and such were the circumstances, and Jesus spoke—a story that may occupy four or five verses, or less. Something happened, Jesus said or did something that impressed his friends, and they could never forget it. The story, as such impressions do, keeps its sharp edges. Date and perhaps even place may be forgotten, but the look and the tone of the speaker are indelible memories. In the experience of every man there are such moments, and the reminiscences can be trusted. The Gospels are almost avowedly not first-hand. Peter is said to be behind Mark; Mark and at least one other are behind Matthew and Luke. Luke in his preface explains his methods. They are collectors and transmitters; and the indications are that they did their work very faithfully.

There is a simplicity and a plainness about the stories in the Gospels, which further guarantees them. It is remarkable how little of the adjective there is—no compliment, no eulogy, no heroic touches, no sympathetic turn of phrase, no great passages of encomium or commendation. It is often said about the Greek historian, Thucydides, that, among his many intellectual judgments, he never offers a criticism of any act that implies moral approbation or disapprobation; that he says nothing to show that he had feelings or that he cared about questions of right and wrong. Page after page of Thucydides will make the reader tingle with pity or indignation; there is hardly in literature so tragic a story as the Syracusan expedition—and the writer did not feel! Is it not the sternest and deepest feeling, after all, when a man will not "unpack his heart with words"? Something of this kind we find in the Gospels. There is not a word of condemnation for Herod or Pilate, for priest or Pharisee; not a touch of sympathy as the nails are driven through those hands; a blunt phrase about the soldiers, "And sitting down they watched him there" (Matt. xxvii. 36)—that is all. (From a literary point of view, what a triumph of awful, quiet objectivity! and they had no such aim.) Luke indeed has one slight touch that might be called irony[1]—"And he released unto them him that for sedition and murder was cast into prison, whom they had desired; but he delivered

[1] *Cf.* the foreigner's touch at Athens (Acts xvii. 21).

Jesus to their will" (Luke xxiii. 25)—and yet the irony is in the story itself. "Why callest thou me good?" So it is recorded that Jesus once answered a compliment (Matt. xix. 17); and it looks as if the mood had passed over to his intimates, and from them to their friends who wrote the Gospels. He meant too much for them to seek the facile relief of praise. The words of praise die away, yes, and the words of affection too; and their silence and self-restraint are in themselves evidence of their truth, and more winning than words could have been.

Here and there the Gospels keep a phrase actually used by Jesus, and in his native Aramaic speech. The Greek was not apt to use or quote foreign phrases—unlike the Englishman who "has been at a great feast of languages and stolen the scraps." Why, then, do the Evangelists, writing for Greek readers, keep the Aramaic sentences? It looks like a human instinct that made Peter—if, as we are told, he had some part in the origination of Mark's Gospel—and the rest wish to keep the very words and tones of their Master, as most of us would wish to keep the accents and phrases of those we love. Was there no satisfaction to the people who had lived with Jesus, when they read in Mark the very syllables they had heard him use, and caught his great accents again? Is there not for Christians in every age a joy and an inspiration in knowing the very sounds his lips framed? The first word that his mother taught him survives in *Abba* (Father)—something of his own speech to let us begin at the beginning; something, again, that takes us to the very heart of him at the end, in his cry: *Eloi, Eloi, lama sabachthani* (Mark xv. 34). Is it not true that we come nearer to him in that cry in the language strange to us, but his own? Would not the story, again, be poorer without the tender little phrase that he used to the daughter of Jairus (Mark v. 41)?

From time to time we find in the Gospels matters for which the writers and those behind them have felt that some apology or at least some explanation was needed. His friendship for sinners was a taunt against him in his lifetime; so was his inattention to the Sabbath (Mark ii. 24, iii. 2), and the details of ceremonial washing (Mark vii. 1-5). The faithful record of these is a sound indication both of the date[1] and of the truth of the Gospels. But these were not all. Celsus, in 178 A.D., in his *True Word*, mocked at Jesus because of the cry upon the cross; he reminded Christians that many and many a worthless knave had endured in brave silence, and their Great Man cried out. It was from the Gospels that his knowledge came (Mark xv. 37). Even during his lifetime the Gospels reveal much about Jesus that in contemporary opinion would degrade him—sighs and tears and fatigue, liability to emotion and to pain, friendship with women.

With these revelations of character we may group passages where the Gospels tell of Jesus surprising or shocking his disciples—startling them by some act or some opinion, for which they were not prepared, or which was contrary to common belief or practice—passages, too, where he blames or criticizes them for conventionality or unintelligence.

[1] Because, later on, the Sabbath and Jewish ceremony were not among the most living issues, after the Church had come to be chiefly Gentile.

It has been remarked that the frequency and fidelity of Jesus' own allusions to country life, his illustrations from bird and beast and flower, and the work of the farm, are evidence for the genuineness of the tradition. Early Christianity, as we see already in the *Acts of the Apostles*, was prevailingly urban. Paul aimed at the great centers of population, where men gathered and from which ideas spread. The language of Paul in his epistles, the sermons inserted by Luke in the *Acts*, writings that survive of early Christians, are all in marked contrast to the speech of Jesus in this matter of country life. When we recall the practice of ancient historians of composing speeches for insertion in their narratives, and weigh the suggestion that the sermons in the *Acts* may conceivably owe much to the free rehandling of Luke or may even be his own compositions, there is a fresh significance in his marked abstention from any such treatment of the words of Jesus. It means that we may be secure in using them as genuine and untouched reproductions of what he said and thought.

This leads us to another point. The central figure of the Gospels must impress every attentive reader as at least a man of marked personality. He has his own attitude to life, his own views of God and man and all else, and his own language, as we shall see in the pages that follow. So much his own are all these things that it is hard to imagine the possibility of his being a mere literary creation, even if we could concede a joint literary creation by several authors writing independent works. Indeed, when we reflect on the character of the Gospels, their origin and composition, and then consider the sharp, strong outlines of the personality depicted, we shall be apt to feel his claim to historicity to be stronger than we supposed.

Finally, two points may be mentioned. The Church from the very start accepted the Gospels. Two of them were written by men in Paul's own personal circle (Philemon 24; Col. iv. 10, 14). All found early acceptance and wide use,[1] and after a century we find Irenæus maintaining that four Gospels are necessary, and are necessarily all—there are four points of the compass, four seasons and so forth; therefore it is appropriate that there are four Gospels. The argument is not very convincing; but that such an argument was possible is evidence to the position of the Gospels as we have them. We must remember the solidarity of that early Church. The constituency, for which the Gospels were written, was steeped in the tradition of Jesus' life, and the Christians accepted the Gospels, as embodying what they knew; and there were still survivors from the first days of the Gospel. When Boswell's *Life of Johnson* was published, the great painter, Sir Joshua Reynolds, a lifelong friend of Johnson, said it might be depended upon as if delivered upon oath; Burke too had a high opinion of the book. In the same way the Gospels come recommended to us by those who knew Jesus, though, it is true, we do not know their names.

The Gospels do not tell us all that Christians thought of Jesus, but they imply more than they say. The writers limited themselves. That Luke, for years a friend of Paul's, so generally kept his great friend's

[1] On this point see R. W. Dale, *The Living Christ and the Four Gospels;* and W. Sanday, *The Gospels in the Second Century.*

theology, above all his Christology, out of his Gospel, is significant. It does not mean divergence of view. More reasonably we may conclude something else: he held to his literary and other authorities, and he was content; for he knew to what the historical Jesus brings men—to new life and larger views, to a series of new estimates of Jesus himself. He left it there. In what follows, we must not forget in our study that behind the Gospels, simple and objective as they are, is the larger experience of the ever-working Christ.

There are three canons which may be laid down for the study of any human character, whether of the past or of to-day. They are so simple that it may hardly seem worth while to have stated them; yet they are not always very easy to apply. Without them the acutest critic will fail to give any sound account of a human character.

First of all, give the man's words his own meaning. Make sure that every term he uses has the full value he intends it to carry, connotes all he wishes it to cover, and has the full emotional power and suggestion that it has for himself. Two quite simple illustrations may serve. The English-born clergyman in Canada who spoke of a meeting of his congregation as a "homely gathering" did not produce quite the effect he intended; "home-like" is one thing in Canada, "homely" quite another, and the people laughed at the slip—they knew, what he did not, that "homely" meant hard-featured and ugly. My other illustration will take us towards the second canon. I remember, years ago, a working-man of my own city talking a swift, impulsive Socialism to me. He was young and something of a poet.

He got in return the obvious common sense that would be expected of a mid-Victorian, middle-aged and middle-class. And then he began to talk of hunger—the hunger that haunted whole streets in our city, where they had indeed something to eat every day, but never quite enough, and the children grew up so—the hunger that he had experienced himself, for I knew his story. With his eyes fixed on me, he brought home to me by the quiet intensity of his speech—whether he knew what he effected or not—that he and I gave hunger different senses. He gave the word for me a new meaning, with the glimpse he gave me of his experience. Since then I have always felt, when men fling theories out like his—schemes, too, like his—wild and impracticable: "Ah, yes! what is at the heart of it all? What but this awful experience which *they* have known and *you* have not—the sight of your own folk hungering, life and faculty wasted for want of mere food, and children growing up atrophied from the cradle"? It is not easy to dissociate the language and the terms of others from the meaning one gives to them oneself; it means intellectual effort and intellectual discipline, a training of a strenuous kind in sympathy and tenderness; but if we are to be fair, it must be done. And the rule applies to Jesus also. Have we given his meaning to his term —force, value, emotion, and suggestion? In a later chapter we shall have to concentrate on one term of his—God—and try to discover what he intends that term to convey.

The second canon is: Make sure of the experience behind the thought. How does a man come to think and feel as he does? That is the question antecedent to any real criticism. What is it that has led him to such a view? It is more important for us to determine that, than to decide at once whether we think him right or wrong. Again and again the quiet and sympathetic study of what a man has been through will modify our judgment upon his conclusions; it will often change our own conclusions, or even our way of thinking. We have, then, to ask ourselves, What is the experience that leads Jesus to speak as he does, to think as he does? In his case, as in every other, the central and crucial question is, What is his experience of God? In other words, What has he found in God? what relations has he with God? what does he expect of God? what *is* God to him? Such questions, if we are candid and not too quick in answering, will take us a long way. It was once said of a man, busy with some labor problem, that he was "working it out in theory, unclouded by a single fact." Is it not fair to say that many of our current judgments upon Jesus Christ are no better founded? Can we say that we have any real, sure, and intimate knowledge of his experience of God? The old commentator, Bengel, wrote at the beginning of his book that a man, who is setting out to interpret Scripture, has to ask "by what right" he does it. What is our right to an opinion on Jesus Christ?

The third canon will be: Ask of what type and of what dimensions the nature must be, that is capable of that experience and of that language. One of the commonest sources of bad criticism is the emphasis on weak points. The really important thing in criticism is to understand the triumphs of the poet or painter, let us say, whom we are studying. How came he to achieve poem or picture, so profound and so true? In what does he differ from other men, that he should do work so fundamental and so eternal? Lamb's punning jest at Wordsworth—that Wordsworth was saying he could have written *Hamlet*, if he had had the mind—puts the matter directly. What is the mind that can do such things? The historian will have to ask himself a similar question about Jesus.

Here we reach a point where caution is necessary. Will the Jesus we draw be an antiquary's Jesus—an archaic figure, simple and lovable perhaps, but quaint and old-world—in blunt language, outgrown? A Galilean peasant, dressed in the garb of his day and place, his mind fitted out with the current ideas of his contemporaries, elevated, it may be, but not essentially changed? A dreamer, with the clouds of the visionaries and apocalyptists ever in his head? When we look at the ancient world, the great men are not archaic figures. Matthew Arnold found in Homer something of the clearness and shrewdness of Voltaire. There is nothing archaic about Plato or Virgil or Paul—to keep abreast of their thinking is no easy task for the strongest of our brains, so modern, eternal, and original they are. They have shaped the thinking of the world and are still shaping it. How much more Jesus of Nazareth! When we make our picture of him, does it suggest the man who has stirred mankind to its depths, set the world on fire (Luke xii. 49), and played an infinitely larger part in all the affairs of men than any man we know of in history? Is it a great figure? Does our emphasis fall on the great features of that nature—are they within our vision, and in our drawing? Does our explanation of him really explain him, or leave him more a riddle? What do we make of his originality? Is it in our picture? What was it in him that changed Peter and James and John and the rest from companions into worshipers, that in every age has captured and controlled the best, the deepest, and tenderest of men? Are we afraid that our picture will be too modern, too little Jewish? These are not the real dangers. Again and again our danger is that we under-estimate the great men of our race, and we always lose by so doing. That we should over-estimate Jesus is not a real risk; the story of the Church shows that the danger has always been the other way. But not to under-estimate such a figure is hard. To see him as he is, calls for all we have of intellect, of tenderness, of love, and of greatness. It is worth while to try to understand him even if we fail. God, said St. Bernard, is never sought in vain, even when we do not find Him. Jesus Christ transcends our categories and classification; we never exhaust him; and one element of Christian happiness is that there is always more in him than we supposed.

CHAPTER II

CHILDHOOD AND YOUTH

It has been remarked as an odd thing by some readers that the Gospels tell us so little of the childhood of Jesus. It must be remembered, however, that they are not really biographies, even of the ancient order—still less of that modern kind, in which the main concern is a tracing of the psychological development of the man. Plutarch, the prince of ancient biographers, put fact and eulogy together, cited characteristic sayings or doings of his hero, quoted contemporary judgments, and wove the whole into a charming narrative, good to read, pleasant to remember, perhaps not without use as a lesson in conventional morality; but with little real historical criticism in it, and as little, or less, attempt at any effective reconstruction of a character. His biography of Pericles illustrates his method and his defects.

The writers of the Gospels did not altogether propose biography as their object either in the ancient or the modern style. They left out—perhaps because it did not survive—much about the life of Jesus that we should like to know. The treatment of Mark by Matthew shows a certain matter-of-fact habit, which explains the obvious want of interest in aspects of the life and mind of Jesus that would to a modern be fascinating. They are dealing with the earthly life of the Son of God —and they deal with it with a faithfulness to tradition and reminiscence, which is, when we really consider it, quite surprising. But it is the heavenward side of the Master that mattered to them most, and it is perhaps not a mere random guess that they were not in any case so aware of the interest of childhood and of children as Jesus was. Matthew and Luke record the miraculous birth, and each adds a story, that has never failed to fascinate men, of the Magi or the Shepherds who came to the manger cradle. Luke gives one episode of Jesus' childhood. That is all.

The writers of the Apocryphal Gospels did their best to fill the gap by inventing or developing stories, pretty, silly, or repellent, which only show how little they understood the original Gospels or the character of Jesus.

But when we turn to the parables of Jesus, and ask ourselves how they came to be what they are, by what process of mind he framed them, and where he found the experience from which one and another of them spring, it is at once clear that a number of them are stories of domestic life, and the question suggests itself, Why should he have gone afield for what he found at home? If we know that he grew up in the ordinary circle of a home, and then find him drawing familiar illustrations from the common scenes of home, the inference is easy that he is going back to the remembered daily round of his own boyhood.

In stray hints the Gospels give us a little of the framework of that boyhood in Nazareth. The elder Joseph early disappears from the story, and we find a reference to four brothers and several sisters. "Is not this the carpenter?" people at Nazareth asked, "the son of Mary, the brother of James and Joseph, and of Judah and Simon?

and are not his sisters here with us?" (Mark vi. 3); Matthew adds a word that may or may not be significant—"his sisters, are they not *all* with us?" (Matt. xiii. 56). In ancient times a particular view of the Incarnation, linked with other contemporary views of celibacy and the baseness of matter, led men to discover or invent the possibility that these brothers and sisters were either the children of Joseph by a former wife, or the cousins of Jesus on his mother's side.[1] That cousins in some parts of the world actually are confused in common speech with brothers may be admitted; but to the ordinary Greek reader "brothers" meant brothers, and "cousins" something different. No one, not starting with the theories of St. Jerome, let us say, on marriage and matter and the decencies of the Incarnation, would ever dream from the Greek narrative of the episode of the critical neighbors at Nazareth, who will not accept Jesus as a prophet because they know his family—a delightfully natural and absurd reason, with history written plain on the face of it—that Jesus had no brothers, only cousins or half-brothers at best. When History gives us brothers, and Dogma says they must be cousins—in any other case the decision of the historian would be clear, and so it is here.

We have then a household—a widow with five sons and at least two, or very likely more, daughters. Jesus is admittedly her eldest son, and is bred to be a carpenter; and a carpenter he undoubtedly was up to, we are told, about thirty years of age (Luke iii. 23). The dates

[1] The reader will see that I am referring to Bishop Lightfoot's article on "The Brethren of the Lord" in his commentary on *Galatians*, but not accepting his conclusions.

of his birth and death are not quite precisely determined, and people have fancied he may have been rather older at the beginning of his ministry. For our purposes it is not of much importance. The more relevant question for us is: How came he to wait till he was at least about thirty years old before he began to teach in public? One suggested answer finds the impulse, or starting-point, of his ministry in the appearance of John the Baptist. It is a simpler inference from such data as we have that the claims of a widowed mother with six or seven younger children, a poor woman with a carpenter's little brood to bring up, may have had something to do with his delay. In any case, the parables give us pictures of the undeniable activities of the household.

A group of parables and other allusions illustrate the life of woman as Jesus saw it in his mother's house. He pictures two women grinding together at the mill (Luke xvii. 35), and then the heating of the oven (Matt. vi. 30)—the mud oven, not unlike the "field ovens" used for a while by the English army in France in 1915, and heated by the burning of wood *inside* it, kindled with "the grass of the field." Meanwhile the leaven is at work in the meal where the woman hid it (Matt. xiii. 33), and her son sits by and watches the heaving, panting mass—the bubbles rising and bursting, the fall of the level, and the rising of other bubbles to burst in their turn—all bubbles. Later on, the picture came back to him—it was like the Kingdom of God—"all bubbles!" said the disappointed, but he saw more clearly. The bubbles are broken by the force of the active life at work beneath—life, not death, is the story. The Kingdom of God is life; the leaven is of more account than any number of bubbles. And we may link all these parables from bread-making with what he says of the little boy asking for bread (Matt. vii. 9)—the mother fired the oven and set the leaven in the meal long before the child was hungry; she looked ahead and the bread was ready. Is not this written also in the teaching of Jesus—"your heavenly Father knoweth that ye have need of all these things" (Matt. vi. 32)? God, he holds, is as little taken aback by his children's needs as Mary was by hers, and the little boys did not confine their demands to bread—they wanted eggs and fish as well (Matt. vii. 10; Luke xi. 11, 12; and *cf.* John vi. 9)—there was no end to their healthy appetites. It is significant that he mentions the price of the cheapest flesh food used by peasants (Luke xii. 6). They also wanted clothes, and wore them as hard as boys do. The time would come when new clothes were needed; but why could not the old ones be patched, and passed down yet another stage? And his mother would smile —and perhaps she asked him to try for himself to see why; and he learnt by experiment that old clothes cannot be patched beyond a certain point, and later on he remembered the fact, and quoted it with telling effect (Mark ii. 21). He pictures little houses (Luke xi. 5-7) and how they are swept (Luke xi. 25)—especially when a coin has rolled away, into a dusty corner or under something (Luke xv. 8); and candles, and bushels (Matt. v. 15), and beds, and moth, and rust (Matt. vi. 19) and all sorts of things that make the common round of life, come into his talk, as naturally as they did into his life.

The carpenter's shop, we may suppose, was close to the house—a shop where men might count on good work and honest work; and what memories must have gathered round it! Is it fanciful to suggest that what the churches have always been saying, about "Coming to Jesus," began to be said in a natural and spontaneous way in that shop? Those little brothers and sisters did not always agree, and tempers would now and then grow very warm among them (*cf.* Luke vii. 32). And then the big brother came and fetched them away from the little house to the shop, and set one of them to pick up nails, and the other to sweep up shavings—to help the carpenter. They helped him. Like small boys, when they help, they got in his road at every turn. But somehow they slipped back to a jolly frame of mind. The big brother told them stories, and they came back different people. I can picture a day when there was a woman in the little house, weary and heavy-laden, and the door opened, and a cheery, pleasant face looked in, and said, "Won't you come and talk to me?" And she came and talked with him and life became a different thing for her. Are these pictures fanciful—mere imagination? Are we to think that all the tenderness of Jesus came to him by a miracle when he was thirty years of age? Must we not think it was all growing up in that house and in that shop? Or did he never tell a story—he who tells them so charmingly—till he wanted parables? We have to note, at the same time, some elements of criticism of the elder brother in the family attitude, some defect of sympathy and failure to understand him, even if kindness prompted their action in later days (Mark iii. 21, 31).

Nazareth lies in a basin among hills, from the rim of which can be seen to the southward the historic plain of Esdraelon, and eastward the Jordan valley and the hills of Gilead, and westward the Mediterranean. On great roads, north and south of the town's girdle of hills, passed to and fro the many-colored traffic between Egypt and Mesopotamia and the Orient. Traders, pilgrims, Herods—"the kingdoms of the world and the glory of them" (Matt. iv. 8)—all within reach, and traveling no faster as a rule than the camel cared to go—they formed a panorama of life for a thoughtful and imaginative boy. More than one allusion to king's clothes comes in his recorded teaching (Matt. vi. 29, xi. 8), and it was here that he saw them—and noticed them and remembered. One is struck with the amount of that unconscious assimilation of experience which we find in his words, and which is in itself an index to his nature. We are not expressly told that he sought the sights that the road afforded; but it would be hard to believe that a bright, quick boy, with genius in him, with poetry in him, with feeling for the real and for life, never went down on to that road, never walked alongside of the caravans and took note of the strange people "from the east and from the west, from the north and from the south" (Luke xiii. 29)—Nubians, Egyptians, Romans, Gauls, Britons, and Orientals.[1] In the one anecdote that survives of his boyhood, we find men "astonished at his understanding" (Luke ii. 47), his gift for putting questions, and his comments on the answers; and all life through he had a genius for friendship.

[1] That this is not quite fanciful is shown by the emphasis laid by more or less contemporary writers on the increased facilities for travel which the Roman Empire gave, and the use made of them.

When we consider how Jesus handles Nature and her wilder children in his parables, another point attracts attention. Men vary a great deal in this. To take two of the Old Testament prophets, we find a marked difference here between Ezekiel and Jeremiah. Ezekiel "puts forth a riddle and speaks a parable" about an eagle—a frankly heraldic eagle, that plants a tree-top in a city of merchants (Ezek. xvii. 2-5). Jeremiah is obviously country-bred. He might have been surprised, if he had been told how often he illustrates his thought from bird and beast and country life—and always with a certain life-like precision and a perfectly clear sympathy.

In the Gospels we find again the same faithfulness to living nature, another country-bred boy with the same love for bird and beast and the wild, open country-side.

> The Earth
> And common face of Nature spake to me
> Remememberable things,[1]

Nature is enough for Jesus as for Jeremiah; she needs no remodeling, no heraldic paints—"long pinions of divers colors"—she will do as she is; she is just splendid and lovable and true as God made her; and she slides into his mind whenever he is deeply moved. Think of all the parables he draws from Nature—the similes, metaphors, and illustrations; every one of them will bear examination and means more the nearer we look into it, and the better we know the living thing behind. The eagle, in Jesus' sentence, plants no trees, but it has the living bird's

[1] Wordsworth, *Prelude*, i. 586.

instinct for carrion; the ancient Greek historian and Lord Roberts at Delhi in 1858 remarked that "wheresoever the body is, thither will the eagles be gathered together" (Luke xvii. 37). In India that year, it was said, they gathered from all over to Delhi. What brought them? Instinct, we say; and we find Jesus, in that rather dark sentence, suggesting somehow that there is an instinct which knows "where." And sheep and cows and asses, and hens and sparrows, and red sunsets, fill men's reminiscences of his talk; and we may safely conclude that, when allusions are so many in fragments of conversation preserved as these are, the man's speech and mind were attuned to the love of bird and beast.

Is there another teacher of those times who is at all so sure that God loves bird and flower? The Greek poet Meleager of Gadara—not so very far removed from Jesus in space of time—has a good deal to say about flowers, but not at all in the same sense as Jesus, not with any feeling such as his for the immortal hand and eye that planned their symmetry, and their colors and sweetness. St. Paul is conspicuously a man of the town—"a citizen of no mean city" (Acts xxi. 39), and he dismisses the animals abruptly (1 Cor. ix. 9); he has hardly an allusion to the familiar and homely aspects of Nature, so frequent and so pleasant in the speech of Jesus. He finds Nature, if not quite "red in tooth and claw," yet groaning together, subject to vanity, in bondage to corruption, travailing in pain, looking forward in a sort of desperate hope to a freedom not yet realized (Rom. viii. 19-24). Nature is far less tragic for Jesus, far happier—perhaps because he knew nature on closer terms of intimacy; Nature, as he portrays things, is in nearer touch with the Heavenly Father than we should guess from Paul,[1] and there is no hint in his recorded words that he held the ground to be under a curse. If we are to use abstract terms and philosophize his thought a little, we may agree that the four facts Jesus notes in Nature are its mystery, its regularity, its impartiality, and its peacefulness.[2] What he finds in Nature is not unlike what Wordsworth also finds—

> A Power
> That is the visible quality and shape
> And image of right reason; that matures
> Her processes by steadfast laws; gives birth
> To no impatient or fallacious hopes,
> No heat of passion or excessive zeal,
> No vain conceits; provokes to no quick turns
> Of self-applauding intellect; but trains
> To meekness, and exalts by humble faith;
> Holds up before the mind intoxicate
> With present objects, and the busy dance
> Of things that pass away, a temperate show
> Of objects that endure.[3]

This is not a passage that one could imagine the historical Jesus speaking, or, still less, writing; but the essential ideas chime in with his observation and his attitude—"for the earth bringeth forth fruit of herself; first the blade, then the ear, after that the full corn in the ear" (Mark iv. 28). Man can count safely on earth's cooperation. From it all, and in it all, Jesus read deep into God's mind and methods.

---

[1] *Cf.* F. G. Peabody, *Jesus Christ and Christian Character*, pp. 57-60.

[2] H. S. Coffin, *Creed of Jesus*, pp. 240-242.

[3] *Prelude* xiii. 26 ff.

It has often been remarked how apt Jesus was to go away to pray alone in the desert or on the hillside, in the night or the early dawn—probably no new habit induced by the crowded days of his ministry, but an old way of his from youth. The full house, perhaps, would prompt it, apart from what he found in the open. St. Augustine, in a very appealing confession, tells us how his prayers may be disturbed if he catch sight of a lizard snapping up flies on the wall of his room (*Conf.*, x. 35, 57). The bird flying to her nest, the fox creeping to his hole (Luke ix. 58)—did these break into the prayers of Jesus—and with what effect? Was it in such hours that he learnt his deepest lessons from the birds and the lilies of the field? Why not? As he sat out in the wild under the open sky, did the stars never speak to him, as to Hebrew psalmist and Roman Virgil?

> When I consider thy heavens, the work of thy fingers,
> The moon and the stars which thou hast ordained;
> What is man, that thou art mindful of him?
> And the son of man, that thou visitest him?
>
> (Psalm viii. 3, 4.)

It is a question men have to meet and face; and if we can trust Matthew's statement, an utterance of his in later years called out by the sneer of a Pharisee, shows how he had made the old poet's answer his own—

> Out of the mouths of babes and sucklings thou hast perfected praise (Matt. xxi. 16).

If this were a solitary utterance of his thought upon Nature, it might be ranked with one or two pointed citations he made of the letter of the Old Testament; but it is safe, perhaps, to take it as one of many indications of his communion with God in Nature. The wind blowing in the night where it listed—must we authenticate every verse of the Fourth Gospel before we believe that he listened to it also and caught something? At any rate, in later years, when his friends are over-driven and weary, quiet and open-air in a desert place are what he prescribes for them and wishes to share with them—surely a hint of old experience (Mark vi. 31).

But now let us turn back to Nazareth, for, as the Gospel reminds us, there he grew up. "The city teaches the man," said the old Greek poet Simonides; and it does, as we see, and more than we sometimes realize. Jesus grew up in an Oriental town, in the middle of its life—a town with poor houses, bad smells, and worse stories, tragedies of widow and prodigal son, of unjust judge and grasping publican — yes, and comedies too. We know at once from general knowledge of Jewish life and custom, and from the recorded fact that he read the Scriptures, that he went to school; and we could guess, fairly safely, that he played with his school-fellows, even if he had not told us what the games were at which they played—

> At weddings and at funerals,
> As if his life's vocation
> Were endless imitation.

Sometimes the children were sulky and would not play (Luke vii. 32). How strange, and how delightful, that the great Gospel, full of God's word for mankind, should have a little corner in it for such reminiscences of children's games! We cannot suppose that he had access to many books, but he knew the Old Testament well and familiarly—better and more aptly than some people expected. Traces of other books have been found in his teaching, not many and some of them doubtful. Generally one would conclude that, apart from the Old Testament, his education was not very bookish—he found it in home and shop, in the desert, on the road, and in the market-place.

It is interesting to gather from the Gospel what Jesus says of the talk of men, and it is surprising to find how much it is, till we realize how very much in ancient times the city was the education, and the market-place the school, where some of the most abiding lessons were learnt. Is it not so still in the East? Here was a boy, however, who watched men and their words more closely than they guessed, on whose ears words fell, not as old coinages, but as new minting, with the marks of thought still rough and bright on them—indexes to the speaker.

Proverbs of the market every people has of its own. "It is nought, it is nought, saith the buyer, but, after he is gone his way, then he boasteth." And the seller has all the variants of *caveat emptor* ready to retort. In antiquity, and in the East to-day, apart from machine-made things, we find the same uncertainty in most transactions as to the value of the article, the same eagerness of both seller and buyer to get at the supposed special knowledge of the other, and the same preliminary skirmish of proposal, protest, offer, refusal, and oath. Jesus stands by the stall, watching some small sale with the bright, earnest eyes which we find so often in the Gospels. The buyer swears "on his head" that he will not give more than so much; then, "by the altar" he won't get the thing. "By the earth" it isn't worth it; "by the heaven" the seller gave that for it. So the battle rages, and at last the bargain is struck. The buyer raises his price; the seller takes less than he gave for the thing; neither has believed the other, but each, as the keen eyes of the onlooker see, feels he has over-reached the other. Heaven has been invoked — and what is Heaven? As the words fell on the listener's ears, he saw the throne of God, and on it One before whose face Heaven itself and earth will flee away—and be brought back again for judgment. And by Heaven, and by Him who sits on the Throne, men will swear falsely for an *anna* or two. How can they? It is because "nothings grow something"; the words make a mist about the thing. In later days Jesus told his followers to swear not at all—to stick to Yes and No.

Then a leader in the religious world passes, and the loiterers have a new interest for the moment. "Rabbi, Rabbi," they say, and the great man moves onward, obviously pleased with the greeting in the market-place (Matt. xxiii. 7). As soon as he is out of hearing, it is no longer "Rabbi" he is called; talk turns to another tune. How little the fine word meant! How lightly the title was given! Worse still, the title will stand between a man and the facts of life. Some will use it to deceive him; others, impressed by it, are silent in his presence; one way and another, the facts are kept from him. Seeing, he sees not, and he comes to live in an unreal world. How many men to-day will say what they really think before a man in clerical dress, or a dignitary however trivial? "Be not ye called 'Rabbi,'" was the counsel Jesus gave to his followers, and he would accept neither "Rabbi," nor "Good Master," nor any other title till he saw how much it meant. "Master!" they said, "we know that thou art true, and teachest the way of God in truth, neither carest thou for any man: for thou regardest not the person of men" (Matt. xxii. 16). But as the evangelist continues, Jesus "perceived their wickedness"—he had heard such things before and was not trapped. "Hosanna in the highest!" (Mark xi. 10)—strange to think of the quiet figure, riding in the midst of the excited crowd, open-eyed and undeceived in his hour of "triumph"—as little perturbed, too, when his name is cast out as evil. How little men's praise and their blame matter, when your eyes are fixed on God—when you have Him and His facts to be your inspiration! On the other hand, when you have not contact with God, how much men's talk counts, and how easy it is to lose all sense of fact!

By the by the talk veers round to what Pilate had done to the Galileans—if the dates fit, or if for the moment we can make them fit, or anticipate once for all, and be done with the bazar talk which never stopped. Pilate had killed the Galileans when they went up to Jerusalem—yes! mingled their own blood, you might say, with the blood of their sacrifices (Luke xiii. 1). What would he do next? There was no telling. What was needed—some time it was bound to come — and the voice sank — a Theudas, or a Judas again (Acts v. 36, 37) — it would not be surprising. . . . There were no newspapers, no approved and reliable sources of news such as we boast to have from our governments and millionaires; all was rumor, bazar talk — "Lo! here!" and "Lo! there!" (Mark xiii. 21). *Prohibiti sermones ideoque plures,* said Tacitus of Rome — rumors were forbidden, so there were more of them. The Messiah *must* come some time, said one man who might be a friend of the Zealots. In any case, reflected another, those Galileans had probably angered Heaven and got their deserts; ill luck like that could hardly come by accident; think of the tower that fell at Siloam — anybody could see there was a judgment in it. Might it not be said that God had discredited John the Baptist, now his head was taken off? So men speculated (*cf.* John ix. 2). Jesus saw through all this, and was radiantly clear about it.

So they chattered, and he heard. Then the talk took another turn, and tales were told—bad eyes flashed and lips smacked, as one story-teller eclipsed the other in the familiar vein. *The Arabian Nights* are tales of the crowd, it is said, rather than literature in their origin, and will give clues enough to what might be told. Jesus heard, and he saw what it meant; and afterwards he told his friends: "From within, out of the heart of men, proceed evil thoughts, adulteries, fornications, murders . . . foolishness; all these evil things come from within, and defile the man" (Mark vii. 21-23). The evil thought takes shape to find utterance, and gains thereby a new vitality, a new power for evil, and may haunt both speaker and listener for ever with its defiling memory.

By and by he intervened and spoke himself. Every one was shocked, and said, "Blasphemy!" They were not used to think of God as he did, and it seemed improper.

Then the whole question of human speech rises for him. What did they mean by their words? What could their minds be like? God dragged in and flung about like a counter, in a game of barter—but if you speak real meaning about God it is blasphemy. "Rabbi, Rabbi" to the great man's face—he turns his back—and his name is smirched for ever by a witty improvisation. Why? Why should men do such things? The magic in the idle tale—ten minutes, and the memory is stained for ever with what not one of them would forget, however he might wish to try to forget. The words are loose and idle, careless, flung out without purpose but to pass the moment—and they live for ever and work mischief. How can they be so light and yet have such power?

Later on he told his friends what he had seen in this matter of words. They come from within, and the speaker's whole personality, false or true, is behind what he says—the good or bad treasure of his heart. There are no grapes growing on the bramble bush. No wonder that of every idle word men shall give account on the day of Judgment (Matt. xii. 36). The idle word — the word unstudied — comes straight from the inmost man, the spontaneous overflow from the spirit within, natural and inevitable, proof of his quality;

and they react with the life that brought them forth.[1]

So he grows up—in a real world and among real people. He goes to school with the boys of his own age, and lives at home with mother and brothers and sisters. He reads the Old Testament, and forms a habit of going to the Synagogue (Luke iv. 16). All points to a home where religion was real. The first word he learnt to say was probably *Abba*, and it struck the keynote of his thoughts. But he knew the world without as well—turned on to it early the keen eyes that saw all, and he recognized what he saw. Knowledge of men, but without cynicism, a loving heart still in spite of his freedom from illusions—these are among the gifts that his environment gave him, or failed to take away from him.

---

[1] See further, on this, in Chapter VII.

CHAPTER III

THE MAN AND HIS MIND

It is a commonplace with those who take literature seriously that what is to reach the heart must come from the heart; and the maxim may be applied conversely—that what has reached a heart has come from a heart — that what continues to reach the heart, among strange peoples, in distant lands, after long ages, has come from a heart of no common make. The Anglo-Saxon boy is at home in the *Odyssey*; and when he is a man—if he has the luck to be guided into classical paths—he finds himself in the *Æneid*; and from this certain things are deduced about the makers of those poems—that they knew life, looked on it with bright, keen eyes, loved it, and lived it over again as they shaped it into verse.

When we turn to the first three Gospels, we find the same thing. Here are books with a more world-wide range than Homer or Virgil, translated again and again from the first century of their existence on to the latest—and then more than ever—into all sorts of tongues, to reach men all over the globe; and that purpose they have achieved. They have done it not so much for the literary graces of the translators or even of the original authors, though in one case these are more considerable than is sometimes allowed. That the Gospels owe their appeal to the recorded sayings and doings of our Lord, is our natural way of putting it to-day; but if for "our Lord" we put a plainer description, more congenial to the day in which the Gospels were written, we shall be in a better position to realize the significance of the world-wide appeal of his words. Thus and thus, then, spoke a mere provincial, a Jew who, though far less conspicuous and interesting, came from the region of Meleager and Philodemos—not from their town of Gadara, nor possibly from their district, but from some place not so very far away.

It was not to be expected that he should win the hearts of men as he did. He had not the Greek culture of the two Gadarenes. Celsus even found his style of speech rather vulgar. But he has, as a matter of common knowledge—so common as hardly to be noted—won the hearts of men in every race and every land. The fact is familiar, but we have as historians and critics to look for the explanation. What has been his appeal? And what the heart and nature, from which came this incredible power and reach of appeal? "Out of the abundance (the overflow) of the heart the mouth speaketh," he said (Matt. xii. 34). This he amplified, as we have seen, by his insistence on the weight of every idle word (Matt. xii. 36) — the unstudied and spontaneous expression or ejaculation—the reflex, in modern phrase—which gives the real clue to the man's inner nature and deeper mind, which "justifies" him, therefore, or "condemns" him (Matt. xii. 37). The overflow of the heart, he holds, shows more decisively than anything else the quality of the spring in its depths.

Here is a suggestion which we find true in ordinary life as well as in the study of literature. If we turn it back upon its author, he at least will not complain, and we shall perhaps gain a new sense of his significance by approaching him at a new angle, from an outlook not perhaps much frequented. How did he come to speak in this manner, to say this and that? To what feeling or thought, to what attitude to life, is this or the other saying due? If he, too, spoke "out of the overflow of his heart"—and we can believe it when we think of the freshness and spontaneity with which he spoke—of what nature and of what depth was that heart?

We can very well believe that much in his speech that was unforgettable to others, he forgot himself. They remembered, they could not help remembering, what he said; but he — no! he said it and moved on, keeping no register of his sayings; and so much the more natural and characteristic they are. Nor would he, like smaller people, be very careful of the form and turn of his speech; it was never set. Certainly he gave his followers the rule *not* to study their language (Mark xiii. 11). Whether or no he had consciously thought it all out, we can see the value of his rule, and how it fits in with his way of life and safeguards it. Under such a rule speech will not be stereotyped; no set form of words will impose itself on the free movement of thought, the mind can and will move of itself unhampered; and when the mind keeps and develops such freedom of movement, it commonly breaks new ground and handles new things. Not to be careful of our speech means for most of us slovenly thinking; but when a man thinks in earnest and takes truth seriously, when he speaks with his eye on his object, his language will not be slovenly, his instinct for fact will keep his speech pure and true. This is what we find in the sayings of Jesus; there is form, but living form, the freedom and grace which the clear mind and the friendly eye communicate insensibly and inimitably to language.

Our task in this chapter is primarily a historical one. From the words of Jesus we have to work back to the type of mind from which they come. There is always danger in such a task. We may forget the wide and living variety of the mind we study; our own minds may not be large enough, nor tender enough, not various, quick and sympathetic in such a degree as to apprehend what we find, to see what it means, and to relate it to itself, detail to whole. How much greater the danger here! While we analyze, we have to remember that the most correct analysis of features or characteristics may easily fail to give us a true idea of the face or the character which we analyze. The whole is more than the sum of its parts. The face and the character have an "integrity," a wholeness. The detail may be of immense value to us, studied as detail; but for the true view the detail, familiar as it may be to us, and dear to us, must be sunk in the general view. Especially is this true of great characters. The "reconstruction of a personality"—to borrow a phrase from some psychologists—is a very difficult matter, even when we are masters of our detail. There is a proportion, a perspective, a balance, a poise about a character—my terms may involve some mixture of metaphors, but if the mixture brings out the complexity and difficulty of our task, it will be justified. Above all there is life, and as a life deepens and widens, it grows complex, unintelligible, and wonderful. It is more so than ever in the case of Jesus. Yet we have to grapple with this great task, if we are to know him, even if here as elsewhere we realize quickly that the beginning of real knowledge is when we grasp how much we do not know, how much there is to know. Attempted in this spirit, a study of the mind of Jesus and his characteristics should help us forward to some further intimacy with him.

The Gospels do not, like some biographies ancient and modern, give a place to the physical characteristics of Jesus. Suetonius in a very short sketch adds the personal aspect of the poet Horace, who, it is true, had led the way by such allusions (*Epist.* i. 4, 15-16), and tells us how Augustus said he was "a squat little pot" (*sessilis obba*). The *Acts of Thekla* in a similar way describe St. Paul's short figure with its suggestion of quickness. But the only personal traits of this sort that I recall in the New Testament are the eyes of Jesus and Paul's way of stretching out a hand when he spoke. In view of this reticence, it is rather remarkable how often the Gospels refer to Jesus "looking." He "looked round about on" the people in the Synagogue, and then — with some suggestion of a pause and silence while he looked, "he saith unto the man" (Mark iii. 5). When Peter deprecated the Cross, we find the same; "when he had turned about and looked on his disciples, he rebuked Peter" (Mark viii. 33). When the rich young ruler came so impulsively to him to ask him about eternal life, Jesus, "looking upon him, loved him"—and we touch there a certain reminiscence of eye-witnesses (Mark x. 21). There are other references of the same kind in the narratives—the look seems to come into the story naturally, without the writers noticing it. There must have been much else as familiar to his friends and companions. They must have known him as we know our friends—the inflections of his voice, his characteristic movements, the hang of his clothes, his step in the dark, and all such things. Did he speak quickly or slowly? or move his hand when he spoke? The teaching posture of Buddha's hand is stereotyped in his images. We are not told such things about Jesus, and guessing does not take us very far. Yet a stanza in one of the elegies written on the death of Sir Philip Sidney may be taken as a far-away likeness of a greater and more wonderful figure — and not lead us very far astray—

> A sweet, attractive kind of grace;
> The full assurance given by looks;
> Perpetual comfort in a face;
> The lineaments of Gospel books.

If we are not explicitly told of such things by the evangelists, they are easily felt in the story. The "paradoxes," as we call them—a rather dull name for them—surely point to a face alive with intellect and gaiety. The way in which, for instance, the leper approaches him, implies the man's eyes fixed in close study on Jesus' face, and finding nothing there to check him and everything to bring him nearer (Mark i. 41). When Mark tells us that he greeted the Syro-Phœnician woman's sally about the little dogs eating the children's crumbs under the table with the reply, "For the sake of this saying of yours . . . ," we must assume some change of expression on such a face as that of Jesus (Mark vii. 29).

We read again and again of the interest men and women found in his preaching and teaching — how they hung on him to hear him, how they came in crowds, how on one occasion they drove him into a boat for a pulpit. It is only familiarity that has blinded us to the "charm" they found in his speech —"they marveled at his words of charm" (Luke iv. 22) — to the gaiety and playfulness that light up his lessons. For instance, there is a little-noticed phrase, that grows very delightful as we study it, in his words to the seventy disciples—"Into whatsoever house ye enter, first say, Peace to this house (the common *salaam* of the East); and if a son of peace be there, your peace shall rest upon it; if not, your *salaam* will come back to *you*" (Luke x. 6). "A son of peace"—not *the* son of peace—what a beautiful expression; what a beautiful idea, too, that the unheeded *Peace!* comes back and blesses the heart that wished it, as if courteous and kind words never went unrewarded! Think again of "Solomon in all his glory" (Matt. vi. 29)—before the phrase was hackneyed by common quotation. Do not such words reveal nature?

A more elaborate and more amusing episode is that of the Pharisee's drinking operations. We are shown the man polishing his cup, elaborately and carefully;

for he lays great importance on the cleanness of his cup; but he forgets to clean the inside. Most people drink from the inside, but the Pharisee forgot it, dirty as it was, and left it untouched. Then he sets about straining what he is going to drink—another elaborate process; he holds a piece of muslin over the cup and pours with care; he pauses—he sees a mosquito; he has caught it in time and flicks it away; he is safe and he will not swallow it. And then, adds Jesus, he swallowed a camel. How many of us have ever pictured the process, and the series of sensations, as the long hairy neck slid down the throat of the Pharisee—all that amplitude of loose-hung anatomy—the hump—two humps—both of them slid down—and he never noticed—and the legs—all of them—with whole outfit of knees and big padded feet. The Pharisee swallowed a camel—and never noticed it (Matt. xxiii. 24, 25). It is the mixture of sheer realism with absurdity that makes the irony and gives it its force. Did no one smile as the story was told? Did no one see the scene pictured with his own mind's eye — no one grasp the humor and the irony with delight? Could any one, on the other hand, forget it? A modern teacher would have said, in our jargon, that the Pharisee had no sense of proportion—and no one would have thought the remark worth remembering. But Jesus' treatment of the subject reveals his own mind in quite a number of aspects.

When he bade turn the other cheek—that sentence which Celsus found so vulgar—did no one smile, then, at the idea of anybody ever dreaming of such an act (Matt. v. 39)? Nor at the picture of the kind brother taking a mote from his brother's eye, with a whole balk of timber in his own (Matt. vii. 5)? Nor at the suggestion of doing two miles of forced labor when only one was demanded (Matt. v. 41)? Nor when he suggested that anxiety about food and clothing was a mark of the Gentiles (Matt. vi. 32)? Did none of his disciples mark a touch of irony when he said that among the Gentile dynasties the kings who exercise authority are called "Benefactors", (Luke xxii. 25)? It was true; Euergetes is a well-known kingly title, but the explanation that it was the reward for strenuous use of monarchic authority was new. Are we to think his face gave no sign of what he was doing? Was there no smile?

We are told by his biographer that Marcus Aurelius had a face that never changed—for joy or sorrow, "being an adherent," he adds, "of the Stoic philosophy." The pose of superiority to emotion was not uncommonly held in those times to be the mark of a sage—Horace's *nil admirari*. The writers of the Gospels do not conceal that Jesus had feelings, and expressed them. We read how he "rejoiced in spirit" (Luke x. 21)—how he "sighed" (Mark vii. 34) and "sighed deeply" (Mark viii. 12)—how his look showed "anger" (Mark iii. 5). They tell us of his indignant utterances (Matt. xxiii. 14; Mark xi. 17)—of his quick sensitiveness to a purposeful touch (Mark v. 30)—of his fatigue (Mark vii. 24; Luke viii. 23)—of his instant response, as we have just seen, to contact with such interesting spirits as the Syro-Phœnician woman and the rich young ruler. Above all, we find him again and again "moved with compassion." We saw the leper approach him, with eyes fixed on the face of Jesus. The man's appeal—"If thou wilt thou canst make me clean"—his misery moves Jesus; he reaches out his hand, and, with no thought for contagion or danger, he touches the leper—so deep was the wave of pity that swept through him—and he heals the man (Mark i. 40-42). It would almost seem as if the touching impressed the spectators as much as the healing. Compassion is an old-fashioned word, and sympathy has a wide range of suggestions, some of them by now a little cold; we have to realize, if we can, how deeply and genuinely Jesus felt with men, how keen his feeling was for their suffering and for their hunger, and at the same moment reflect how strong and solid a nature it is that is so profoundly moved. Again, when we read of his happy way in dealing with children, are we to draw no inference as to his face, and what it told the children? Finally, on this part of our subject, we are given glimpses of his dark hours. The writer to the Hebrews speaks of his "offering up prayers and supplications with strong crying and tears" and "learning obedience by the things that he suffered" (Heb. v. 7, 8), and Luke, perhaps dealing with the same occasion, says he was "in agony" (Luke xxii. 44), a strong phrase from a man of medical training. Luke again, with the other evangelists, refers to the temptations of Jesus, and in a later passage records the poignant and revealing sentence—"Ye are they that have continued with me in my temptations" (Luke xxii. 28). Finally, there is the last cry upon the Cross (Mark xv. 37). So frankly, and yet so unobtrusively, they lay bare his soul, as far as they saw it.

From what is given us it is possible to go further and see something of his habits of mind. His thought will occupy us in later chapters; here we are concerned rather with the way in which his mind moves, and the characteristics of his thinking.

First of all, we note a certain swiftness, a quick realization of a situation, a character, or the meaning of a word. Men try to trap him with a question, and he instantly "recognizes their trickery" (Luke xx. 23). When they ask for a sign, he is as quick to see what they have in mind (Mark viii. 11-13). He catches the word whispered to Jairus—half hears, half divines it, in an instant (Mark v. 36). He is surprised at slowness of mind in other men (Matt. xv. 16; Mark viii. 21). And in other things he is as quick—he sees "the kingdoms of the world in a moment of time" (Luke iv. 5); he beholds "Satan fallen (aorist participle) from heaven like lightning" (Luke x. 18)—two very striking passages, which illuminate his mind for us in a very important phase of it. We ought to have been able to guess without them that he saw things instantly and in a flash—that they stood out for him in outline and color and movement there and then. That is plain in the parables from nature, and here it is confirmed. Is there in all his parables a blurred picture, the edges dim or the focus wrong? The tone of the parables is due largely to this gift of visualizing, to use an ugly modern word, and of doing it with swiftness and precision.

Several things combine to make this faculty, or at least go along with it—a combination not very common even among men of genius—an unusual sense of fact, a very keen and vivid sympathy, and a gift of bringing imagination to bear on the fact in the moment of its discovery, and afterwards in his treatment of the fact.

On his sense of fact we have touched before, in dealing with his close observation of Nature. It is an observation that needs no note-book, that is hardly conscious of itself. There is, as we know, a happy type of person who sees almost without looking, certainly without noticing—and sees aright too. The temperament is described by Wordsworth in the opening books of *The Prelude*. The poet type seems to lose so much and yet constantly surprises us by what it has captured, and sometimes hardly itself realizes how much has been done. The gains are not registered, but they are real and they are never lost, and come flashing out all unexpectedly when the note is struck that calls them. So one feels it was with Jesus' intimate knowledge of Nature—it is not the knowledge of botanist or naturalist, but that of the inmate and the companion, who by long intimacy comes to know far more than he dreams. "Wise master mariners," wrote the Greek poet, Pindar, long before, "know the wind that shall blow on the third day, and are not wrecked for headlong greed of gain." They know the weather, as we say, by instinct; and instinct is the outcome of intimacy, of observation accurate but sub-conscious.

It chimes in with this instinct for fact, that Jesus should lay so much emphasis on truth of word and truth of thought. Any hypocrisy is a leaven (Matt. xvi. 12; Luke xii. 1); any system of two standards of truth spoils the mind (Matt. v. 33-37). The divided mind fails because it is not for one thing or the other. If it is impossible to serve God and mammon, truth and God go together in one allegiance; and a non-Theocentric element in a man's thought will be fatal sooner or later to any aptitude he has by nature for God and truth.

We find this illustrated in Jesus' own case. At the heart of his instinct for fact is his instinct for God. He goes to the permanent and eternal at once in his quest of fact, because his instinct for God is so sure and so compelling. Bishop Phillips Brooks noted in Jesus' conversation "a constant progress from the arbitrary and special to the essential and universal forms of thought," "a true freedom from fastidiousness," "a singular largeness" in his intellectual life. The small question is answered in the larger—"the life is more than meat and the body is more than raiment" (Luke xii. 23). When he is challenged on divorce, he goes past Moses to God (Matt. xix. 4)—"He which made them at the beginning made them male and female." Every question is settled for him by reference to God, and to God's principles of action and to God's laws and commands; and God, as we shall see in a later chapter, is not for him a conception borrowed from others, a quotation from a book. God is real, living, and personal; and all his teaching is directed to drive his disciples into the real; he insists on the open mind, the study of fact, the fresh, keen eye turned on the actual doings of God.

When life and thought have such a center, a simplicity and an integrity follow beyond what we might readily guess. "When thine eye is single, thy whole body also is full of light, . . . if thy whole body therefore be full of light, having no part dark, the whole shall be full of light, as when the bright shining of a candle doth give thee light" (Luke xi. 34-36). It is this fulness of light that we find in Jesus; and as the light plays on one object and another, how clear and simple everything grows! All round about him was subtlety, cleverness, fastidiousness. His speech is lucid, drives straight to the center, to the principle, and is intelligible. We may not see how far his word carries us, but it is abundantly plain that simple and straightforward people do understand Jesus—not all at once, but sufficiently for the moment, and with a sense that there is more beyond. His thought is uncomplicated by distinctions due to tradition and its accidents. His whole attitude to life is simple—he has no taboos; he comes "eating and drinking" (Matt. xi. 19); and he told his followers, when he sent them out to preach, to eat what they were given (Luke x. 7); "give alms," he says, "of such things as ye have; and, behold, all things are clean unto you" (Luke xi. 41). If God gives the food, it will probably be clean; and the old taboos will be mere tradition of men. He is not interested in what men call "signs," in the exceptional thing; the ordinary suffices when one sees God in it. One of Jesus' great lessons is to get men to look for God in the commonplace things of which God makes so many, as if Abraham Lincoln were right and God did make so many common people, because he likes them best. The commonest flowers—God thinks them out, says Jesus, and takes care of them (Matt. vi. 28-30). Hence there is little need of special machinery for contact with God—priesthoods, trances, visions, or mystical states—abnormal means for contact with the normal. When Jesus speaks of the very highest and holiest things, he is as simple and natural as when he is making a table in the carpenter-shop. Sense and sanity are the marks of his religion.

"Sense of fact" is a phrase which does not exclude—perhaps it even suggests—some hint of dulness. The matter-of-fact people are valuable in their way, but rarely illuminative, and it is because they lack the imagination that means sympathy. Now in Jesus' case there is a quickness and vividness of sympathy—he *likes* the birds and flowers and beasts he uses as illustrations. They are not the "natural objects" with which dull people try to brighten their pages and discourses. They are happy living things that come to his mind, as it were, of themselves, because, shall we say? they know they will be welcome there; and they are welcome. His pity and sympathy are unlike ours in having so much more intelligence and fellow-feeling in them. He understands men and women, as his gift of bright and winning speech shows. After all, as Carlyle has pointed out in many places, it is this gift of tenderness and understanding, of sympathy, that gives the measure of our intellects.[1] It is the faculty by which men touch fact and master it. It is the want of it that makes so many clever and ingenious people so futile and distressing.

The sense of fact and the gift for sympathy are the foundations, so to speak, of the imagination which gives their quality to the stories and pictures of Jesus. He thinks in pictures, as it were; they fill his speech, and every one of them is alive and real. Think, for example, of the Light of the world (Matt. v. 14), the strait gate and the narrow way (Matt. vii. 14), the pictures of the bride-

[1] *E.g.* in his essay on *Mirabeau*: "The real quantity of our insight . . . depends on our patience, our fairness, lovingness"; and in *Biography*: "A loving heart is the beginning of all knowledge."

groom (Mark ii. 19), sower (Matt. xiii. 3), pearl merchant (Matt. xiii. 45), and the men with the net (Matt. xiii. 47), the sheep among the wolves (Matt. x. 16), the woman sweeping the house (Luke xv. 8), the debtor going to prison accompanied by his creditor and the officer with the judge's warrant (Luke xii. 58), the shepherd separating his sheep from the goats (Matt. xxv. 32), the children playing in the market-place pretending to pipe or to mourn (Luke vii. 32), the fall of the house (Matt. vii. 27)—or the ironical pictures of the blind leading the blind straight for the ditch (Matt. xv. 14), the vintagers taking their baskets to the bramble bushes (Matt. vii. 16), the candle burning away brightly under the bushel (Matt. v. 15; Luke xi. 33), the offering of pearls to the pigs (Matt. vii. 6)—or his descriptions of what lay before himself as a cup and a baptism (Mark x. 38), and of his task as the setting fire to the world (Luke xii. 49). There is a truthfulness and a living energy about all these pictures—not least about those touched with irony.

There are, however, pictures less realistic and more imaginative—one or two of them, in the language of the fireside, quite "creepy." Here is a house—a neat, trim little house—and for the English reader there is of course a garden or a field round it, and a wood beyond. Out of the wood comes something—stealthily creeping up towards the house—something not easy to make out, but weary and travel-stained and dusty—and evil. A strange feeling comes over one as one watches—it *is* evil, one is certain of it. Nearer and nearer to the house it creeps—it is by the window—it rises to look in, and one shudders to think of those inside who suddenly see *that* looking at them through the window. But there is no one there.

Fatigue changes to triumph; caution is dropped; it goes and returns with seven worse than itself, and the last state of the place is worse than the first (Luke xi. 24-26). Is this leaving the real? One critic will say it is. "No," says another man, in a graver tone and speaking slowly, "it's real enough; it's my story." But have we left the text too far? Then let us try another passage. Here is a funeral procession, a bier with a dead man laid out on it, "wrapped in a linen cloth" (Matt. xxvii. 59), "bound hand and foot with grave-clothes" (John xi. 44)—a common enough sight in the East; but who are they who are carrying him—those silent, awful figures, bound like him hand and foot, and wound with the same linen cloth, moving swiftly and steadily along with their burden? It is the dead burying the dead (Luke ix. 60). Add to these the account of the three Temptations—stories in picture, which must come from Jesus himself, and illustrate another side of his experience. For to the mind that sees and thinks in pictures, temptation comes in pictures which the mind makes for itself, or has presented to it and at once lights up—pictures horrible and once seen hard to forget and to escape. No wonder he warns men against the pictures they paint themselves in their minds (Matt. v. 28; *cf.* Chapter VII., p. 154). Add also the other pictures of Satan fallen (Luke x. 18) and Satan pushing into God's presence with a demand for the disciples (Luke xxii. 31). Are we to call these "visions" —the word is ambiguous—or are they imaginative presentments of evil, as it thrusts itself on the soul, with all its allurements and all its ugliness? "Visions," in the sense that is associated with trance, we shall hardly call them. They are pictures showing his gift,

Lastly, on this part of our subject, let us remind ourselves of the many parables and pictures and sayings which put God himself before us. Here is the bird's nest, and one little sparrow fallen to the ground—and God is there and he takes notice of it; he misses the little bird from the brood (Matt. x. 29; *cf.* Luke xii. 6). Here again is quite another scene—the rich and middle-aged man, who has prospered in everything and is just completing his plans to retire from business, when he feels a tap on his shoulder and hears a voice speaking to him, and he turns and is face to face with God (Luke xii. 20). And there are all the other stories of God's goodness and kindness and care; is not the very phrase "Our Father in heaven" a picture in itself, if we can manage to give the word the value which Jesus meant it to carry? When one studies the teaching of Jesus, and concentrates on what he draws us of God, God somehow becomes real and delightful, in a most wonderful way.

With all these faculties brought to bear on all he thinks, and lucent in all he says, there is little wonder that men recognized another note in Jesus from that familiar in their usual teachers. Rabbi Eliezer of those times was praised as "a well trough that loses not a drop of water." We all know that type of teacher—the tank-mind, full, no doubt, supplied by pipes, and ministering its gifts by pipe and tap, regulated, tiresome, and dead. "The water that I shall give him," says Jesus in the Fourth Gospel (John iv. 14), "shall be in him a well of water springing up into everlasting life." The water metaphors of the New Testament are not of trough and tank. Jesus taught men—not from a reservoir of quotations, like a scribe or a Rabbi, "but as possessed of authority himself" (Matt. vii. 29). Who gave him that authority? asked the priests (Matt. xxi. 23)? Who authorizes the living man to live? "All things are delivered unto me of my Father" (Matt. xi. 27). "My words shall not pass away" (Mark xiii. 31).

He has proved right; his words have not passed away. The great "Son of Fact," he went to fact, drove his disciples to fact, and (in the striking phrase of Cromwell) "spoke *things*." And we can see in the record again and again the traces of the mental habits and the natural language of one who habitually based himself on experience and on fact. Critics remark on his method of using the Old Testament, and contrast it with contemporary ways. St. Paul, for instance, in the passage where he weighs the readings "seeds" and "seed" (Gal. iii. 16), is plainly racking language to the destruction of its real sense; no one ever would have written "seeds" in that connection; but in the style of the day he forces a singular into an utterly non-natural significance. St. Matthew in his first two chapters proves the events, which he describes, to have been prophesied by citing Old Testament passages—two of which conspicuously refer to entirely different matters, and do not mean at all what he suggests (Matt. ii. 15, 23). The Hebrew with the Old Testament, like the Greek of those days with Homer, made what play he pleased; if the words fitted his fancy, he took them regardless of connection or real meaning; if he was pressed for a defence, he would take refuge in allegory. A fashion was set for the Church which bore bad fruit. The Old Testament was emptied of meaning to fortify the Christian faith with "proof texts." When Jesus quotes the Old Testament, it is for other ends and with a clear, incisive sense of the prophet's meaning. "Go ye and learn what that meaneth, I will have mercy and not sacrifice" (Matt. ix. 13 and xii. 7, quoting Hosea vi. 6). He not merely quotes Hosea, but it is plain that he has got at the very heart of the man and his message. Similarly when he reads Isaiah in the Synagogue at Nazareth (Luke iv. 17), he lays hold of a great passage and brings out with emphasis its value and its promise. He touches the real, and no lapse of time makes his quotations look odd or quaint. When he is asked which is the first commandment of all, he at once, with what a modern writer calls "a brilliant flash of the highest genius," links a text in Deuteronomy with one in Leviticus—"Hear, O Israel; The Lord our God is one Lord, and thou shalt love the Lord thy God with all thy heart, and with all thy soul, and with all thy mind, and with all thy strength" (Deut. vi. 4-5), and, he adds, "the second is like, namely this, Thou shalt love thy neighbour as thyself. There is none other commandment greater than these" (Levit. xix. 18; Mark xii. 29–31). Thus his instinct for God and his instinct for the essential carry him to the very center and acme of Moses' law. At the same time he can use the Old Testament in an efficient way for dialectic, when an *argumentum ad hominem* best meets the case (Mark vii. 6; Luke xx. 37, 44).

Going to fact directly and reading his Bible on his own account, he is the great pioneer of the Christian habit of mind. He is not idly called the Captain by the writer to the Hebrews (Heb. ii. 10, xii. 2). Authority and tradition only too readily assume control of human life; but a mind like that of Jesus, like that which he gave to his followers, will never be bound by authority and tradition. Moses is very well, but if God has higher ideas of marriage—what then? The Scribes and the Pharisees sit in Moses' seat (Matt. xxiii. 2), but that does not make them equal to Moses; still less does it make their traditions of more importance than God's commandments (Mark vii. 1-13). The Sabbath itself "was made for man, and not man for the Sabbath" (Mark ii. 27).

Where the habit of mind is thus set to fact, and life is based on God, on God's will and God's doings, it is not surprising that in the daily round there should be noted "sanity, reserve, composure, and steadiness." It may seem to be descending to a lower plane, but it is worth while to look for a moment at the sheer sense which Jesus can bring to bear on a situation. The Sabbath—is it lawful to heal on the Sabbath? Well, if a man's one sheep is in a pit on the Sabbath, what will he do? (Matt. xii. 11), or will he refrain from leading his ox to the water on a Sabbath (Luke xiii. 15)? Such questions bring a theological problem into the atmosphere of sense—and it is better solved there. He is interrupted by a demand that he arbitrate between a man and his brother; and his reply is virtually, Does your brother accept your choice of an arbitrator? (Luke xii. 14)—and that matter is finished. "Are there few that be saved?" asks some one in vague speculation, and he gets a practical answer addressed to himself (Luke xiii. 23). Even in matters of ordinary manners and good taste, he offers a shrewd rule (Luke xiv. 8). Luke records also two or three instances of perfectly banal talk and ejaculation addressed to him—the bazar talk of the Galilean murders (Luke xiii. 1; *cf.* Chapter II., p. 37)—the pious if rather obvious remark of some man about feasting in the Kingdom of

God (Luke xiv. 15)—and the woman's homely congratulation of Mary on her son (Luke xi. 27). In each case he gets away to something serious.

Above all, we must recognize the power which every one felt in him. Even Herod, judging by rumor, counts him greater than John the Baptist (Matt. xiv. 2). The very malignity of his enemies is a confession of their recognition that they are dealing with some one who is great. Men remarked his sedative and controlling influence over the disordered mind (Mark i. 27). He is not to be trapped in his talk, to be cajoled or flattered. There is greatness in his language—in his reference of everything to great principles and to God; greatness in his freedom from ambition, in his contempt of advertisement and popularity, in his appeal to the best in men, in his belief in men, in his power of winning and keeping friends, in his gift for making great men out of petty. In all this we are not stepping outside the Gospels nor borrowing from what he has done in nineteen centuries. In Galilee and in Jerusalem men felt his power. And finally, what of his calm, his sanity, his dignity, in the hour of betrayal, in the so-called trials, before the priests, before Pilate, on the Cross? The Pharisees, said Tertullian, ought to have recognized who Christ was by his patience.

CHAPTER IV

THE TEACHER AND THE DISCIPLES

It was as a teacher that Jesus of Nazareth first began to gather disciples round him. But to understand the work of the Teacher, we must have some general impression of the world to which he came. The background will help us understand what had to be done, and what it was that he meant to do.

Bishop Gore, in a book recently published, suggested that the belief that God is Love is not axiomatic. Many of us take it for granted, as the point at which religion naturally begins; but, as he emphasized, it is not an obvious truth; it is something of which we have to be convinced, something that has to be made good to men. Unless we bear this in mind, we shall miss a great deal of what Jesus has really done, by assuming that he was not needed to do it.

"Out of a darker world than ours came this new spring." We must look at the world as it was, when Jesus came. In a later chapter we shall have to consider more fully the religions of the Roman world. One or two points may be anticipated. First of all, we have to realize what a hard world it was. Men and women are harder than we sometimes think, and the natural hardness to which the human heart grows of itself, needed more correction than it had in those days. Among the many papyrus documents that have been found in late years in Egypt—

documents that have pictured for us the life of Egypt, and have recorded for us also the language of the New Testament in a most illuminative way—there is one that illustrates only too aptly the unconscious hardness of the times. It is a letter—no literary letter, no letter that any one would ordinarily have thought of keeping; it has survived by accident. It was written by an Egyptian Greek to his wife. She lived somewhere up the country, and he had gone to Alexandria. She had been expecting a baby when he left, and he wrote a rough, but not an unkind, letter to her. He writes: "Hilarion to Alis . . . greetings. . . . Know that we are still even now in Alexandria. Do not fidget, if, at the general return, I stay in Alexandria. I pray and beseech you, take care of the little child, and as soon as we have our wages, I will send you up something. If you are delivered, if it was a male, let it live; if it was a female, cast it out. . . . How can I forget you? So don't fidget."[1] The letter is not an unkind one; it is sympathetic, masculine, direct, and friendly. And then it ends with the suggestion, inconceivable to us to-day, that if the baby is a girl, it need not be kept. It can be put out either on the land or in the river, left to kite or crocodile. The evidence of satirists is generally to be discounted, because they tend to emphasize the exceptional; and it is not the exceptional thing that gives the character of an age, or of a man. It is the kind of thing that we take for granted and assume to be normal that shows our character or gives the note of the day; and what we omit to notice may be as revealing. In the plays of the Athenian comic poets

[1] *Cf.* Deissmann, *Light from the Ancient East,* p. 154. I have omitted one or two less relevant clauses—*e.g.* greetings to friends.

of the third and fourth centuries B.C. we find to wearisomeness one recurring plot. The heroine turns out to be, not just a common girl, but the daughter of the best family in Athens, exposed when she was a baby. When Plato sketched his ideal constitution, in addition to the mating of suitable pairs to be decided by government, he added that, if the offspring were not good enough, it should be put away where it would not be found again. Aristotle allowed the same practice. The most cultured race on earth freely exposed its infants; and this letter of Hilarion to Alis—a dated letter by the way, of September or October in the year 1 A.D.—makes it clear that the practice of exposure of children still prevailed; and there is other evidence which need not now detain us. It is a hard world, where kind people or good people can think of such things as ordinary and natural.

Evidence of the character of an age is given by the treatment of criminals; and that age was characterized by crucifixion. They would take a human being, spread him out on a cross on the ground, drive nails through his hands and feet; and then the cross was raised—the agony of the victim during the movement is not to be imagined. It was made fast; and there the victim hung, suspended between heaven and earth, to live or die at his leisure. By and by crows would gather round him. "I have been good," said the slave. "Then you have your reward," says the Latin poet, "you will not feed the crows on the cross."[1] There is a very striking phrase in St. Matthew: "And sitting down they watched him there" (Matt. xxvii. 36). The soldiers nailed three men to crosses, and sat down beneath them to dice for their

[1] Horace, *Epistles*, i. 16, 48.

clothes. Our tolerances, like our utterances, come out of the abundance of the heart, and stamp us for what we are.

We cannot easily realize all that slavery meant. When we read in the Fourth Gospel that "the Lamb of God taketh away the sin of the world" (John i. 29), that was written before Jesus Christ had abolished slavery; for, we remember, it was done by his people against the judgment of the business experts. Slavery meant robbing the man of every right that Nature gave him; and, as Homer said long ago, "Farseeing Zeus takes away half a man's manhood, when he brings the day of slavery upon him."[1] He became a thief, a liar, dirty, and bad; and with the woman it was still worse. The slave woman was a little lower than the animal; she might not have offspring. It was "natural," men said; "Nature had designed certain races to be slaves; slavery was written in Nature; it was Nature's law." These were not the thoughts of vulgar people, but of some of the best of the Greeks—not of all, indeed; but society was organized on the basis of slavery. It was an accepted axiom of all social and economic life.

As to the spiritual background, for the present let us postpone the heathen world and consider the Jews, who represented in some ways the world's highest at this period. Modern scholarship is shedding fresh light on the literature and ideas that were prevalent between the end of the Old Testament and the beginning of the New. But what uncertainty about God! Why some people should think that it was easier to believe in God in those days than now, I do not see. Far less was known

[1] Homer, *Odyssey*, xvii. 322.

of God; the record of his doings was not so long as it is for us, and it was not so well known. No one could understand what God meant, if he was quite clear himself. Look at what he did with the nation. He chose Israel, he established the kingdom of David. They did not get on very well, and at last were carried away into captivity in Babylon. So much he did for his people; and when he brought them back again to the Promised Land, it was to a very trying and difficult situation; and worse still followed after Nehemiah's day. Alexander the Great's conquest of the East left a Macedonian dynasty ruling those regions, and one of their great kings, Antiochus Epiphanes, tried to stamp out the religion of Jehovah altogether. The Book of Daniel is a record of that persecution about 166 B.C. The Maccabæan brothers delivered Israel, and rescued the religion of Jehovah; and a kingdom of a sort was established with them; but the grandsons of the liberators became tyrants. What did God mean? Out of all the promises to Israel, to the House of David, this is what comes. Herod follows—a foreign king and an Edomite; and the Romans are over all, suzerains and rulers.

In despair of the present men began to forecast the future. A time will surely come, they said, when God will give an anointed one, the Messiah; he will set all Israel free, will make Israel rule the world instead of the Romans; he will gather together the scattered of Israel from the four winds, reunite and assemble God's people in triumph in Palestine. And then, when the prophet paused, a plain man spoke: "I don't care if he does. My father all his life looked forward to that. What does it matter now, if God redeems his people, or if he does not? My father is dead." The answer was, why should your father not come with the redeemed Israel? But what evidence is there for that? Does God care for people beyond the grave? Is there personal immortality?—that became the anxious question.[1]

But is this kingdom of the Messiah to be an earthly or a heavenly kingdom? Will it be in Jerusalem or in heaven? Are you quite sure that there is any distinction in the other world between good and bad, between Jew and Gentile? Some people thought the kingdom would be in Jerusalem; others said it would be in heaven, and added that the Jews will look down and see the Gentiles in hell—something worth seeing at last. But, after all, it was still guesswork—"perhaps" was the last word.

When the question is asked, "Was Jesus the Messiah?" the obvious reply is, "Which Messiah?" For there seems to have been no standard idea of the Messiah. The Messiah was, on the whole, as vague a term as, in modern politics, Socialism or Tariff Reform. Neither of them has come; perhaps they never will come, and nobody knows what they will be till they do come. Jesus is not what they expected. A Jewish girl, at an American Student Conference a year or two ago, said about Jesus: "I do not think he is the Messiah, but I do love him." Of course he was not in her Jewish sense. The term was a vague one. The main point was that men were uncertain about God. God was unintelligible. They did not understand his ideas, either for the nation or for the

[1] It is only about four times that personal immortality comes with any clearness in the Old Testament: Psalms lxxii. and cxxxix.; Isaiah xxvi.; and Job xix. 26.

individual; God's plans miscarried with such fatality. Or if he had some deeper design, it was still all guess-work. It seemed likely, or at least right, that he should achieve somehow the final damnation of the Gentiles—the Romans, and the rest of us—but nothing was very clear. In the meantime, if God was going to damn the Gentiles in the next world, why should not the Jews do it in this? Human nature has only too ready an answer for such a question—as we can read in too many dark pages of history, in the stories of wars and religious persecutions.

The uncertainty about God in Judaism reacted on life and made it hard.

Even the virtues of men were difficult; they were apt to be nerveless and uncertain, because their aim was uncertain, and they wanted inspiration. Of course there are always kindly hearts; but a man will never put forth quite his best for an uncertainty. There was a want of center about their virtues, a want of faith, and as a result they were too largely self-directed.[1] A man was virtuous in order to secure himself in case God should be awkward. There was no sufficient relation between man and God. God was judge, no

---

[1] *Cf.* A. E. J. Rawlinson, *Dogma, Fact and Experience,* p. 16. "All the virtues in the Aristotelian canon are self-contained states of the virtuous man himself. . . . In the last resort they are entirely self-centered adornments or accomplishments of the good man; and it is significant of this self-centeredness of the entire conception that the qualities of display (*megaloprepeia*) and high-mindedness, or proper pride (*megalopsychia*), are insisted on as integral elements of the ideal character. On the other hand, the three characteristic Christian virtues—faith, hope and charity—all postulate Another."

doubt; but his character could be known from his attitude to the Gentiles. Could a man count on God and how far? Could he rely on God supporting him, on God wishing to have him in this world and the next? No, not with any certainty. It comes to a fundamental unbelief in God, resting, as Jesus saw, on an essential misconception of God's nature; and this resulted in the spoiling of life. Men did not use God. "Where your treasure is, there will your heart be also," Jesus said (Luke xii. 34); and it was not in God. Men's interest and belief were elsewhere.

Now the first thing that Jesus had to do, as a teacher, was to induce men to rethink God. Men, he saw, do not want precepts; they do not want ethics, morals or rules; what they do need is to rethink God, to rediscover him, to re-explore him, to live on the basis of relation with God. There is one striking difference between Christianity and the other religions, in that the others start with the idea that God is known. Christians do not so start. We are still exploring God on the lines of Jesus Christ—rethinking God all the time, finding him out. That is what Jesus meant us to do. If Jesus had merely put before men an ethical code, that would have been to do what the moralists had done before him—what moralists always do, with the same naïve idea that they are doing a great deal for us. His object was far more fundamental.

The first thing was to bring people on to the very center and to get there at once—to get men away from the accumulation of occasional and self-directed virtues, from the self-sustained life, from self-acquired righteousness, and to bring them to face the fact of God, to realize the seriousness of God and of life, and to see God. When he preached self-denial, he did not mean the modern virtue of self-denial with all its pettinesses, but a genuine negation of self, a total forgetfulness of self by having the mind set entirely on God and God's purposes, a readjustment of everything with God as the real center of all. This is always difficult; it is not less difficult where the conception of God is, as it was with Jesus, entirely spiritual. The whole experience of mankind was against the idea that there could be a religion at all without priest, sacrifice, altar, temple, and the like. There is a very minimum of symbol and cult in the teaching of Jesus—so little that the ancient world thought the Christians were atheists, because they had no image, no temple, no sacrifice, no ritual, nothing that suggested religion in the ordinary sense of the word. We shall realize the difficulty of what Jesus was doing when we grasp that he meant people to see God independently of all their conventional aids. To lead them to commit themselves in act to God on such terms was a still more difficult thing. To believe in God in a general sort of way, to believe in Providence at large, is a very different thing from getting yourself crucified in the faith that God cares for you, and yet somehow wishes you to endure crucifixion. How far will men commit themselves to God? Jesus means them to commit themselves to God right up to the hilt—as Bunyan put it, "to hazard all for God at a clap." Decision for God, obedience to God, that is the prime thing—action on the basis of God and of God's care for the individual.

His purpose that this shall not be merely the religion of choice spirits or of those immediately around him, but shall be the one religion of all the world, makes the task still vaster. He means not merely to touch the Jews. Whether he says so in explicit terms or not, it is implied in all that he says and does, that the new movement should be far wider than anything the world had ever seen; it was to cover the whole of mankind. He meant that every individual in all the world should have the center of gravity of his thinking shifted.

Again, he had to think of a re-creation of the language of men, till God should be a new word. Our constant problem is to give his word his value, his meaning. He meant that men should learn their religious vocabulary again, till the words they used should suggest his meanings to their minds. Something of this was achieved, when some of his disciples came to him and said: "Teach us to pray, as John also taught his disciples" (Luke xi. 1). Further, he had to secure that men should begin the rethinking of all life—personal, social, and national—from the very foundations, on new lines—what is called a transvaluation of all values. With a new center, everything has to be thought out anew into what St. Paul calls the fulness of Christ (Eph. iv. 13). Then finally the question comes, how to secure continuity? Will the movement outlast his personal influence? These are his problems—large enough, every one of them. How does he face them?

The Gospel began with friendship, and we know from common life what that is, and how it works. Old acquaintance and intimacy are the heart of it. The mind is on the alert when we meet the stranger—quick and eager to master his outlook and his ways of thought, to see who and what he is—it is critical, self-protective, rather than receptive. But, as time goes on, we notice less, we study the man less as we see more of him. Yet, in this easier and more careless intercourse, when the mind is off guard, it is receiving a host of unnoticed impressions, which in the long run may have extraordinary influence. Pleasant and easy-going, a perpetual source of interest and rest of mind, the friendship continues, till we find to our surprise that we are changed. Stage by stage, as one comes to know one's friend, by unconscious and freely given sympathy, one lives the other man's life, sees and feels things as he does, slips into his language, and, by degrees, into his thoughts—and then wakes up to find oneself, as it were, remade by the other's personality, so close has been the identification with the man we grew to love. This is what we find in our own lives; and we find it in the Gospels.

A sentence from St. Augustine's *Confessions* gives us the key to the whole story. *Sed ex amante alio accenditur alius* (*Confessions,* iv. 14, 21). "One loving spirit sets another on fire." Jesus brings men to the new exploration of God, to the new commitment of themselves to God, simply by the ordinary mechanism of friendship and love. This, in plain English, is after all the idea of Incarnation—friendship and identification. Jesus has a genius for friendship, a gift for understanding the feelings of men. Look, for example, at the quick word to Jairus. As soon as the message comes to him that his daughter is dead, Jesus wheels round on him at once with a word of courage (Mark v. 36). This quickness in understanding, in feeling with people, marks him throughout. An instinctive care for other people's small necessities is a great mark of friendship, and Jesus has it. We find him saying to his disciples: "Come ye yourselves apart privately into a desert place, and rest awhile" (Mark vi. 31). What a beautiful suggestion! He himself, it is clear from the records, felt the need of privacy, of being by oneself, of quiet; and he took his quiet hours in the open, in the wild, where there was solitude and Nature, and there he would take his friends. There were so many coming and going, that they had no leisure to eat, and Jesus says to them in his friendly way: "Let us get out of this—away by ourselves, to a quiet place; what you want is rest." What a beautiful idea!—to go camping out on the hillside, under the trees, to rest—and with him to share the quiet of the lonely place. It is not the only time when he offers to give people rest—"Come unto Me . . . and I will give you rest" (Matt. xi. 28). How strange, when one thinks of the restless activity of Christian people to-day, with typewriters and conventions, and every modern method of consuming energy and time! How sympathetic he is!

We may notice again his respect for the reserve of other people. On the whole, how slowly Jesus comes to work with men! He never "rushes" the human spirit; he respects men's personalities. Men and women are never pawns with him. He does not think of them in masses. The masses appeal to him, but that is because he sees the individual all the time. To one of his disciples he says, "I have prayed for *thee*" (Luke xxii. 32). What a contrast to the conventional "friend of man" in the abstract! With all that hangs upon him, he has leisure to pray intensely, for a single man. It gives us an idea of his gifts in friendship. His faith in his people is quite remarkable, when we think of it. He believes in his followers; he shares with them some of the deepest things in his life; he counts them fit to share his thought of God. He makes it quite clear to them how he trusts them. He puts before them the tremendous work that he has to do—work more appalling in its vastness the more one studies it; and then he tells them that he is trusting the whole thing with them. What a faith it implies in their moral capacity! What acceptance of the dim beginnings of the character that was to be Christian! Someone has spoken of his "apparently unjustified faith in Peter." What names he can give to his friends as a result of this faith in them! "Ye are the light of the world," he says (Matt. v. 14), "the salt of the earth." When we remind ourselves of his clear vision, his genius for seeing fact, how much must such praises have meant to these men!

Think how he gives himself to them in earnest; how he is at their disposal. He is theirs; they can cross-question him at leisure; they tell him that the Pharisees did not like what he said (Matt. xv. 12), they doubt with Peter the wisdom of his open speech (Mark viii. 32); they criticize him (Matt. xiii. 10). If they do not understand his parable, they ask what he means (Matt. xv. 15) and keep on asking till he makes it plain. He is in no hurry. He is the Master and their Teacher, and he is at the service of the slowest of them.

But there is another side to friendship; for one great part of it is taking what our friends do for us, as well as doing things for them. How he will take what they have to give! He lets them manage the boat, while he sleeps (Mark iv. 38), and go and prepare for him

(Luke ix. 52), and see to the Passover meal (Mark xiv. 13). The women, we read, ministered to him of their substance (Luke viii. 3). There is a very significant phrase in St. Luke (xxii. 28), where he says to them at the end: "Ye are they that have continued with me in my temptations." He tells them there that they have helped him. How? Apparently by being with him. Is not that friendship? In the same chapter (Luke xxii. 15) we find an utterance that reveals the depth of his feeling for his friends: "With desire I have desired (a Greek rendering of a Semitic intensive) to eat this passover with you before I suffer." They are to help him again by being with him, and he has longed for it, he says. The Gospel of John sums up the whole story in a beautiful sentence: "Jesus, having loved his own which were in the world, loved them unto the end" (John xiii. 1). Augustine is right. "One loving spirit sets another on fire."

Note again the word which he uses in speaking to them (*Tekna*: Mark ii. 5, x. 24). It is a diminutive, a little disguised as "children" in our English version. It reappears in the Fourth Gospel in even more diminutive forms (*Teknia*, xiii. 33; *Paidia*, xxi. 5) with a peculiarly tender suggestion. The word of Mark answers more closely than anything I know to "Boys," as we used it in the Canadian Universities. "Men," or "Undergraduates," is the word in the English Universities; "Students," in Scotland and in India; in Canada we said "Boys"; and I think we get nearer, and like one another better, with that easy name. And it was this friendly, pleasant word, or one very like it, that he used with them. Nor is it the only one of the kind. "Fear not, little flock!" he said (Luke xii. 32). Do not the diminutives mean something? Do they not take us into the midst of a group where friendship is real? And in the center is the friendliest figure of all.

Look for a moment at the men who followed him; at the type he calls. They are simple people in the main—warm hearts and impulsive natures. The politics of Simon the Zealot might at one time have been summed up as "the knife and plenty of it," a simple and direct enough type of political thought, in all conscience, however hopeless and ineffectual, as history showed; but he gave up his politics for the friendship of Jesus. Peter, again, is the champion example of the impulsive nature. Why Jesus called James and John "the sons of thunder" (Mark iii. 17) I am not sure. Dr. Rendel Harris thinks because they were twins; other people find something of the thunderstorm in their ideas and outlook. The publican in the group is of much the same type; he is ready to leave his business and his custom-house at a word—once more the impulsive nature and the simple. It is possible that Jesus looked also to another type of which he gained very little in his lifetime; for he speaks of "the scribe who has turned disciple again, and brings out of his treasure things new and old" (Matt. xiii. 52)—the more complicated type of the trained scholar, full of old learning, but open to new views. In the meantime he draws to him people with the warm heart—yes, he says, but cultivate the cool head (*cf.* Matt. x. 16). Again and again he will have men "count the cost" (Luke xiv. 28)—know what they are doing, be rid of delusions before they follow him (Mark viii. 34). What did they expect? They had all sorts of dreams of the future. When we first find them, there is friction among them, which is not unnatural in a group of men with ambitions (Mark ix. 33. x. 37). Even at the Last Supper their minds run on thrones (Luke xxii. 24). They are haunted by taboos. Peter long after boasts that nothing common or unclean has entered his lips (Acts x. 14). They fail to understand him. "Are ye also without understanding?" he asks, not without surprise (Mark viii. 17, 21). At the very end they run away.

There, then, is the group. What is to be the method? There is not much method. As Harnack says about the spread of the early Church, "A living faith needs no special methods"—a sentence worth remembering. "Infinite love in ordinary intercourse" is another phrase of Harnack in describing the life of the early Church. It began with Jesus. He chose twelve, says Mark (iii. 14), "that they may be with him." That is all. And they are with him under all sorts of circumstances. "The Son of Man hath not where to lay his head" (Luke ix. 58). They saw him in privation, fatigued, exhausted. With every chance to see weaknesses in his character, they did not find much amiss with him. That is surely significant. They lived with him all the time, in a genuine human friendship, a real and progressive intimacy. They were with him in popularity and in unpopularity; they were with him in danger, when Herod tried to kill him and he went out of Herod's territory. But friendship depends not only on great moments; it means companionship in the trivial, too, it means idle hours together, partnership in commonplace things—meals and garden-chairs as well as books and crises. Ordinary life, ordinary talk, gossip, chat, every kind of conversation about Herods and Roman governors, and the Zealots—custom-house memories, tales of the fishermen's life on the lake, stories of neighbors and home—rumors about the Galileans who were murdered by Pilate (Luke xiii. 1-4)—all the babbling talk of the bazar is round Jesus and his group, and some of it breaks in on them; and his attitude to it all is to these men a constant revelation of character. They are with him in the play of feelings, with him in the fluxes and refluxes of his thought—learning his ways of mind without realizing it. They slip into his mind and mood, by a series of surprises, when they are imagining no such thing. Anything, everything serves to reveal him. They tramp all day, and ask some village people to shelter them for the night. The villagers tell them to go away. The men are hungry and fatigued. "What a splendid thing it would be, if we could do like Elijah and burn them up with a word!" So the hot thought rose. He turned and said, "You know not what manner of spirit you are of."—What a gentle rebuke! "The Son of Man is not come to destroy men's lives, but to save them" (Luke ix. 51-56). Then follows one of the wonderful sentences of the Gospel, "they went unto another village"—very obvious, but very significant. A missionary from China told me how, thirty years ago or more, he was driven out of the town where he lived; how the gentlefolk egged on the mob, and they wrecked his house, and hounded him out of the place. He told me how it felt—the misery and the indignity of it. Jesus took it undisturbed. He taught a lesson in it which the Church has never forgotten.

Their life was full of experiences shared with him. He has his reserve—his secret; yet, in another sense, he gives himself to them without reserve; there is prodigality of self-impartation in his dealings with them. He lets them have everything they can take. He becomes theirs in a great intimacy, he gives himself to them. Why? Because he believes, as he put it, in seed. Socrates saw that the teacher's real work, his only work, is to implant the idea, like a seed; an idea, like a seed, will look after itself. A king builds a temple or a palace. The seed of a banyan drifts into a crack, and grows without asking anyone's leave; there is life in it. In the end the building comes down, but for what the banyan holds up. The leaven in the meal is the most powerful thing there. There is very little of it, but that does not matter; it is alive (Matt. xiii. 33). Life is a very little thing, but it is the only thing that counts. That is why the farmer can sow his fields and sleep at nights without thinking of them; and the crop grows in spite of his sleeping, and he knows it (Mark iv. 26). That is why Jesus believes so thoroughly in his men, and in his message; God has made the one for the other, and there is no fear of mischance.

Look at his method of teaching. People "marveled at his words of charm" (Luke iv. 22)—"hung about him to hear him" (Luke xix. 48). He said that the word is the overflow of the heart. "Out of the abundance of the heart the mouth speaketh" (Matt. xii. 34; Luke vi. 45). What a heart, then, his words reveal! How easy and straightforward his language is! To-day we all use abstract nouns to convey our meaning; we cannot do without words ending in *-ality* and *-ation*.

But there is no recorded saying of Jesus where he uses even "personality." He does not use abstract nouns. He sticks to plain words. When he speaks about God he does not say "the Great First Cause," or "Providence," or any other vague abstract. Still less does he use an adverb from the abstract, like "providentially." He says, "your heavenly Father." He does not talk of "humanity"; he says, "your brethren." He has no jargon, no technical terms, no scholastic vocabulary. He urges men not to over-study language; their speech must be simple, the natural, spontaneous overflow of the heart.[1] Jesus told his disciples not to think out beforehand what they would say when on trial (Mark xiii. 11)—it would be "given" to them. He was perfectly right; and when Christians obeyed him, they always spoke much better than when they thought out speeches beforehand. They said much less for one thing, and they said it much better. Take the case of the martyr—an early and historical one—whose two speeches were during her trial *Christiana sum* and, on her condemnation, *Deo gratias*.

With this remark his own gift of arresting phrase; the freshness of his language, how free it is from quotation, how natural and how extraordinarily simple. Everything worth while can be put in simple language; and, if the speech is complicated, it is a call to think again. "As a woman over-curiously trimmed is to be mistrusted, so is a speech," said John Robinson of Leyden, the minister of the Pilgrim Fathers. The language of Jesus is simple and direct, the inevitable expression of a rich

[1] *Cf.* Chapter II., p. 39.

nature and a habit of truth. You feel he does not strain after effect—epigram, antithesis, or alliteration. Of course he uses such things—like all real speakers—but he does not go out of his way for them. No, and so much the more significant are such characteristic antitheses as: "Ye cannot serve God and mammon" (Luke xvi. 13), and "Whosoever will save his life shall lose it" (Matt. xvi. 25), coming with a spontaneous flash, and answering in their sharpness to the sharp edges of fact. His words caught the attention, and lived in the memory; they revealed such a nature; they were so living and unforgettable.

Remark once again his preference for the actual and the ordinary. There are religions in which holiness involves unusual conditions and special diet. Some forms of mysticism seem to be incompatible with married life. But the type of holiness which Jesus teaches can be achieved with an ordinary diet, and a wife and five children. He had lived himself in a family of eight or nine. It is perhaps harder, but it is a richer sanctity, if the real mark of a Saint is, as we have been told, that he makes it easier for others to believe in God. In any case the ordinary is always good enough with Jesus. Only he would have men go deeper, always deeper. Why can you not think for yourselves? he asks. Signs were what men demanded. He pictures Dives' mind running on signs even in hell (Luke xvi. 27). "What could you do with signs? Look at what you have already. You read the weather for to-morrow by looking at the sky to-day. The south wind means heat; the red sky fair weather. Study, look, think" (Luke xii. 55). His animals, as we saw, are all real animals; it is real observation; real analogy. When he speaks of the lost sheep, it is not a fictitious joy that he describes or an imaginary one; it is real. The more we examine his sayings with any touch of his spirit, the more we wonder. Of course it is possible to handle them in the wrong way, to miss the real thought and make folly of everything. Thus, when he says he is the door, the interpreter may stray into silly detail and make faith the key, and—I don't know what the panels and hinges could be. That is not the style of Jesus. The soul of the thing, the great central meaning, the real analogy is his concern. Seriousness in observation, seriousness in reflection, is what he teaches. Men and women break down for want of thinking things out. Many things become possible to those who think seriously, as he did—and, so to speak, without watertight compartments.

Jesus is always urging seriousness in reflection. Seriousness in action, too, is one of his lessons—an emphasis on *doing*, but on doing with a clear sense of what one is about, and why. A part of action is clear thought; always exactness, accuracy; you must think the thing out, he says, and then act or let it alone. The artistic temperament, we all know, is very much in evidence to-day. In *The Comments of Bagshot* we are told that the drawback is that there is so much temperament and so little art. Why? Because the artistic temperament means so little by itself. It is one of the secrets of Jesus, that it is action that illuminates. What is it that makes the poem? The poet sees beggar children running races, or little Edward and the weather-cock, or something greater if you like—the light on a woman's hair, or a flower; and you say, he has his poem. He has not.

He must work at the thing. When we study the great poets, we realize how these things are worked out to the point of nerve-strain and exhaustion. The poet devotes himself heart and soul to the work; he alters this and that, once and again; he sees a fresh aspect of the thing, and he alters all again; he writes and rewrites, getting deeper and deeper into the essential values of the thing all the time. Where in all this is the artistic temperament? It gave him the impulse, but something else achieves the work of art. I have a feeling that the great works of art are achieved by the shopkeeper virtues in addition to the artistic temperament that sees and feels them at the beginning. It is action that gives the value of a thought. Jesus sees that. He says that frankly to his disciples. If you want to understand in the long run, it is carrying the cross that will teach you the real values.

I have been treating him almost as if he were an authority on pedagogy. Fortunately, he never discussed pedagogy, never used the terms I have been using. But he dealt with men, he taught and he influenced them, and it is worth our study to understand how he did it—to master his methods. "One loving spirit sets another on fire." As for the effects of his words at once, as Seeley put it, they were "seething effervescence . . . broodings, resolutions, travail of heart." Men were brought face to face with a new issue; it was a time of choice; things would not be as they were—men must be "with him or against him"—must accept or reject the new teaching, the new teacher, the new life. As he said, "I came to send fire on the earth" (Luke xii. 49), to divide families, to divide the individual soul against itself, till the great choice was made; and so it has always been, where men have really seen him. We have to notice further the transformation of the disciples, who definitely accepted him. "Very wonderful to me," wrote Phillips Brooks, "to see how the disciples caught his method." The promise was made to them that they should become fishers of men (Mark i. 17), and it was fulfilled. Jesus made them strong enough to defy the world and to capture the world. There is something attractive about them; they have his secret, something of his charm; they are magnetic with his power. A new impulse to win men marks them, a new power to do it, a new faith which grows in significance as you study it—the faith of William Carey, a hundred years ago, was the same thing—a perfectly incredible faith, that they actually will win men for God and Christ. And they did—and along his lines and by his methods of love—even for Gentiles. "Woe is me, if I preach not the Gospel," says St. Paul (1 Cor. ix. 16), who to preach the Gospel shipwrecked his life and suffered the loss of all things (Phil. iii. 8). But these men are sure that it is worth while. They have a new passion for men and women—an interest not merely in the saving of their souls but in every real human need. The early Church made a point of teaching men trades when they had none. They learnt all this from him. The greatest miracle in history seems to me the transformation that Jesus effected in those men. Everything else in Christian or secular history, compared to it, seems easy and explicable; and it was achieved by the love of Jesus.

The Church spread over the world without social machinery. The Gospel was preached instinctively, naturally. The earliest Christians were persecuted in Jerusalem, and were driven out. I picture one of them in flight; on his journey he falls in with a stranger. Before he knows what he is doing, he is telling his fellow traveler about Jesus. It follows from his explanation of why he is on the road; he warms up as he speaks. He never really thought about the danger of doing so. And the stranger wants to know more; he is captured by the message, and he too becomes a Christian. And then this involuntary preacher of the Gospel is embarrassed to learn that the man is a Gentile; he had not thought of that. I think that is how it began—so naturally and spontaneously. These people are so full of love of Jesus that they are bound to speak (Acts viii. 4). "One loving heart sets another on fire."

CHAPTER V

THE TEACHING OF JESUS UPON GOD

It is worth taking some trouble to realize how profoundly Jesus has changed the thinking of mankind about God. "Since Jesus lived," Dr. Fairbairn wrote, "God has been another and nearer Being to man." "Jesus," writes Dr. Fosdick, "had the most joyous idea of God that ever was thought of." That joyous sense of God he has given to his followers, and it stands in vivid contrast with the feelings men have toward God in the other religions. Christianity is the religion of joy. The New Testament is full of it.

We know the general character of Jesus' attitude to God, his feeling for God, his sense of God's nearness. How immediate his knowledge of God is, how intimate! Of course, here, as everywhere, his teaching has such an occasional character—or else the records of it are so fragmentary—that we must not press the absence of system in it; and yet, I think, it would be right to say that Jesus puts before us no system of God, but rather suggests a great exploration, an intimacy with the slow and sure knowledge that intimacy gives. He has no definition of God,[1] but he assumes God, lives on the basis of God, interprets God; and God is discovered in his acts and his relations. He said to Peter, in effect—for the familiar

[1] A French mystic is quoted as saying, "Le Dieu défini est le Dieu fini."

phrase comes to this in modern English: "You think like a man; you don't think like God" (Mark viii. 33). Elsewhere he contrasts God's thoughts with man's—their outlooks are so different—"that which is highly esteemed among men is abomination in the sight of God" (Luke xvi. 15; the Greek words are very interesting). In other words, he would have men see all things as God sees them. That we do not so see them, remains the weak spot in our thinking. What Luther said to Erasmus is true of most of us: "Your thoughts concerning God are too human." "Blessed are the pure in heart, for they shall *see* God," said Jesus (Matt. v. 8), and throughout he emphasizes that the vision of God depends on likeness to God—it is love and a glowing purity that give that faculty, rather than any power of intellect apart from them. Jesus brings men back to the ultimate fact. Our views are too short and too narrow. He would have us face God, see him and realize him—think in the terms of God, look at things from God's point of view, live in God and with God. In modern phrase, he breaks up our dogmatism and puts us at a universal point of view to see things over again in a new and true perspective.

How and where did he begin himself? Whence came his consciousness of God, his gift for recognizing God? We do not know. The story of his growth, his inward growth, is almost unrevealed to us. We are told that he learnt "by the things which he suffered" (Heb. v. 8), and that he "increased in wisdom and stature, and in favor with God and man" (Luke ii. 52). Where *does* anyone begin, who takes us any great distance? It is very hard to know. Where did our own thoughts of God begin? What made them? How did they come? There is an inherited element in them, but how much else? Whence came the inherited element? How is it that to another man, with the same upbringing as ours, everything is different, everything means more? Remark, at any rate, in the teaching of Jesus, that there is no mysticism of the type so much studied to-day. There is nothing in the least "psychopathic" about him, nothing abnormal—no mystical vision of God, no mystical absorption in God, no mystical union with God, no abstraction, nothing that is the mark of the professed mystic. Yet he speaks freely of "seeing God"; he lives a life of the closest union with God; and God is in all his thoughts. A phrase like that of Clement of Alexandria, "deifying into apathy we become monadic," is seas away from anything we find in the speech of Jesus. That is not the way he preaches God. He is far more natural; and that his followers accepted this naturalness, and drew him so, and gave his teaching as he gave it, is a fresh pledge of the truthfulness of the Gospels.

Again, his knowledge of God is not a matter of quotation, as ours very often tends to be. He is conscious always of the real nearness of God. He seems to wonder how it is that man can forget God. We do forget God. Augustine in his *Confessions* (iv. 12, 18) has to tell us that "God did not make the world and then go away." The practical working religion of a great many of us rests on a feeling that God is a very long way off. Our practical steps betray that we half think God did go away, when he had made the world. Prayer to us is not a real thing—it is not intercourse face to face; far too often it is like conversation over a telephone wire of infinite length which gets out of order. Even if words travel along that wire, there is so much "buzzing" that they are hardly recognizable. No, says Jesus, God is near, God is here—so near, that Jesus never feels that men have any need of a priesthood to come between, or to help them to God; God does all that. There is no common concern, no matter of food or clothing, no mere detail of the ordinary round of common duty and common life—father and mother, son, wife, friend—nothing of all that, but God is there; God knows about it; God is interested in it; God has taken care of it; God is enjoying it. How is it that men can "reject the counsel of God," refuse God's plans and ideas (Luke vii. 30)? How is it that they forget God altogether? Jesus is surprised at the dullness of men's minds (Mark viii. 17); it is a mystery to him. The rich fool, as we call him, though it is hard to see why *we* should call him a fool, when he is so like ourselves, had forgotten God somehow, and was startled when God spoke, and spoke to him. That story, seen so often among men,—the story of the thorns choking the seed (Matt. xiii. 22)—makes Jesus remark on the difficulty which a rich man finds in entering into the kingdom of God.

God knows—that is what Jesus repeats, God cares; and God can do things; his hands are not tied by impotence. The knowledge of God is emphasized by Jesus; "Even the very hairs of your head are all numbered" (Matt. x. 30); "your Father knoweth" (Luke xii. 30); "seeth in secret" (Matt. vi. 4); "knoweth your hearts" (Luke xvi. 15); knows your struggles, knows your worries, knows your worth; God knows all about you. And "all things are possible with God" (Matt. xix. 26). There is nothing that he cannot do, nothing that he will not do, for his children. Will a father refuse his child bread; will God not give what is good? (Matt. vii. 11). Is it too big a thing for the Giver of Life to give food—which is the more difficult thing to give? (Luke xii. 23). Look at God, as Jesus draws him—interested in flowers; God takes care of them, and thinks about their colors, so that even "Solomon in all his glory" is not equal to them (Matt. vi. 30). God knows the birds in the nest—knows there is one fewer there to-day than there was yesterday (Matt. x. 29). God cares for them; how much more will he care for you (Matt. vi. 26)? "Ye are of more value than many sparrows" (Matt. x. 31). And God thinks out man's life in all its relations, and provides for it. Society moves on lines he laid down for it; his plans underlie all. Thus, when Jesus is challenged on the question of marriage and divorce, with that clear thought and eye of his, he goes right back to God's intent—not to man's usage, not to the common law and practice of nations, but to God's intent and God's meaning. God ordained marriage; he thought it out (Matt. xix. 4). Marriages will be better, if we think of them in this way. God gave men their food, does still, and all things that he gives are clean (Luke xi. 41). We cannot have taboos at our Father's table.

Over all is God's throne (Matt. xxiii. 22). That idea, it seems to me, lapses somehow from our minds to-day. When Luther had to face the hostility of the Kaiser, the Emperor Charles V., he wrote to one of his friends: "Christ comes and sits at the right hand—not of the Kaiser, for in that case we should have perished long ago—but at the right hand of God. This is a great and incredible thing; but I enjoy it, incredible as it is;

some day I mean to die in it. Why should I not live in it?" So Luther wrote—in not quite our modern vein. We hardly calculate on God as a factor; we omit him. Jesus did not. God's rule is over all; and in all our perplexity, doubt, and fear, Jesus reminds us that the first thing is faith in God. The fact is that "Thine is the Kingdom" means peace; it is a joyous reminder. For if he speaks of the Kingdom of God, the King is more than the Kingdom. It is the Kingdom, the rule, of the God whom Jesus teaches us to trust and to love. The Father is supreme. But that has more aspects than one. If our Father is supreme for us, he is supreme over us. Jesus emphasizes the will of God—God's commandment against man's tradition, God's will against man's notions (Mark vii. 8). What a source of rest and peace to him is the thought of God's will! When Dante writes: "And His will is our peace," it is the thought of Jesus. And at the same time God's judgments are as real to Jesus' mind. "I will tell you," he says, "whom to fear, God—yes, fear him!" (Luke xii. 5). He feels the tenderness and the awfulness of God at once.

In speaking of God, it is noticeable that Jesus chiefly emphasizes God's interest in the individual, as giving the real clue to God's nature. On the whole, there is very little even implied, still less explicit, in the Gospels, about God as the great architect of Nature—hardly anything on the lines familiar to us in the Psalms and in Isaiah—"The sea is his, and he made it; and his hands formed the dry land" (Psalm xcv. 5)—"He taketh up the isles as a very little thing" (Isaiah xl. 15). There is little of this in the Gospels; yet it is implied in the affair of the storm (Matt. viii. 26). The disciples in their anxiety wake him. He does not understand their fear. Whose sea is it? Whose wind is it? Whose children are you? Cannot you trust your Father to control his wind and his sea? Of course it is possible that he said more about God as the Author of Nature than our fragmentary reports give us; but it may be that it is because the emphasis on God's care and love for the individual is hardest to believe and at the same time best gives the real value of God, that Jesus uses it so much. Perhaps the Great Artificer is too far away for our minds. He is too busy, we think; and yet, after all, if God is so great, why should he be so busy? If he is a real Father, why should not he be at leisure for his children? He is, says Jesus; a friend has leisure for his friends, and a father for his children; and God, Jesus suggests, always has leisure for you.

The great emphasis with Jesus falls on the love of God. Thus he tells the story of the impossible creditor with two debtors (Luke vii. 42). One owed him ten pounds, and the other a hundred. When they had nothing to pay, they both came to him and told him so. The ordinary creditor, at the very best, would say: "Well, I suppose I must put it down as a bad debt." Jesus says that this creditor took up quite another attitude. He smiled and said to his two troubled friends: "Is that all? Don't let anything like that worry you. What is that between you and me?" He forgave them the debt with such a charm (*echarisato*), Jesus says, that they both loved him. One feels that the end of the story must be, that they both paid him and loved him all the more for taking the money. What a delightful story of charm, and friendship and forgiveness! And it is a true picture of God, Jesus would have us believe, of God's forgiveness and the response it wakes in men.

If we do not definitely set our minds to assimilate the ideas of Jesus, we shall make too little of the heart of God. With Jesus this is the central and crucial reality. He emphasizes the generosity of God. God makes his sun rise on the good and on the bad; he sends rain on the just and the unjust (Matt. v. 45). God's flowers are just as beautiful in the bad man's garden. God knows what his child needs, and gives it, whether it is a very good child or a very bad one. The Father is the same great wise Friend in either case. The peacemakers are recognized as the children of God, because of their family likeness to God (Matt. v. 9). They come among people, and find them in discord with one another, and their presence stills that; or they come into a man's life, when it is all in disorder and pain, and they bring peace there. They may not quite know it, but they do these things almost without meaning to do them. And Jesus says that this is a family likeness by which men know they are God's children. But it is not every teacher, pagan or Christian, who lays such stress on God's gift of peace, or is so sure of it. He uses Hosea's great saying about God—"I will have mercy and not sacrifice" (Hosea vi. 6), as giving the truth about God. Matthew represents him as quoting it twice (Matt. ix. 13, xii. 7); and we can well believe that he found in it the real spirit of God and often referred to it. His own heart has taken him to the tenderest of the utterances of the Old Testament spoken by the most suffering of the Prophets. "Love your enemies," he says (Matt. v. 44); yes, for then you will be the real children of God. Or he speaks of the great patience of God, how God gives every man all the time and all the chance that he needs—sometimes, he half suggests, even a little more. Look at the parable of the fig tree, how the gardener pleads for the tree, begs and obtains another chance for it (Luke xiii. 8); that is like God, says Jesus.

It is easy enough to talk in a vague way about the love of God. But the love of God implies surely the individual; love has little content indeed if its object is merely a collective noun, an abstract, a concept. But that God loves individual men is very difficult for us to believe in earnest. The real crux comes when the question rises in a man's own heart, "Does God love *me?*" Jesus says that he does, but it is very hard to believe, except in the company of Jesus and under his influence. Jesus throughout asserts and reasserts the value of the individual to God. Look, for example, at the picture he draws, when he tells of the recovery of the Lost Sheep, and brings out the analogy. At the end of the Book of Job (ch. xxxviii.) the poet carries his reader back to the first sight of a world new-made, and tells how God, like the real artist and creator—we might not have thought of all this, but the poet did—loves his work so much that he must have his friends sharing it with him. He calls them; he shows them the world he has made—"the beauty, and the wonder, and the power," as Browning says. The poet tells us that what followed was that "the morning stars sang together, and all the sons of God shouted for joy." The sight was so good that song and shout came instinctively, almost involuntarily. Is it not the same picture which Jesus draws of "joy in heaven in the presence of the angels of God over one sinner that repenteth"? We can believe in such joy when God made the world; but can we believe that there was the same joy in the presence of God yesterday when a coolie gave his heart to God? Jesus does. That is the central thing, it seems to me, in his teaching about God—that God cares for the individual to an extent far beyond anything we could think possible. If we can wrestle with that central thought and assimilate it, or, as the old divines said, "appropriate" it, make it our own, the rest of the Gospel is easy. But one can never manage it except with the help, and in the company, of Jesus.

Jesus goes a step further, and believes in the possibility of a man loving God and God enjoying that too. If he speaks of prayer must we not think he means that God wants it as much as his child can want it? How much is involved in the name "Father," which Jesus so uniformly gives to God? Something less than the word carries in the case of a human father, or more? What is the attitude of a father to his child? Jesus, as we have seen, uses this illustration to bring out God's care for the actual needs of his children. But is that all? What is the innermost thing in a father's relation to his children? Surely something more than the bird's instinct to feed her young, or to gather them under her wings (Luke xiii. 34). Is not one of the most real features of parenthood enjoyment of the child? Do not men and women frankly enjoy the grappling of the little mind with big things? Is there not a charm, as says one of the Christian Fathers (Minucius Felix), about the "half-words" that a child uses, as he learns to talk and wrestles with a grown-up vocabulary? About the extraordinary pictures he will draw of ships or cows—the quaint stories he will invent—the odd ways in which his gratitude and his affection express themselves? Is it a real fatherhood where such things do not appeal? Jesus' language about God, his whole attitude to God, implies throughout that God is as real a Father as anybody, and it suggests that God loves his children the more because they are real; because they are not very clever; because they do make such queer and imperfect prayers; because, in short, they need him; and because they fill a place in his heart.

We have to remark how firmly Jesus believes in his Gospel of God and man needing each other and finding each other—his "good news," as he calls it. He bases all on his faith in what has been called "Man's incurable religious instinct"—that instinct in the human heart that must have God—and in God's response to that instinct which he himself implanted, and which is no accident found here and missing there, but a genuine God-given characteristic of every man, whatever his temperament or his range in emotions may be, his swiftness or slowness of mind. The repeated parables of seed and leaven—the parables of vitality—again and again suggest his faith in his message, his conviction that God must have man and man must have God—that, as St. Augustine puts it, "Thou hast made us for Thyself, and our heart knows no rest till it rests in Thee" (*Conf.*, i. 1). That is the essence of the Gospel.

How this union of the soul with God comes about, Jesus does not directly say, but there are many hints in his teaching that bear upon it. "The Kingdom of Heaven cometh not with observation," he said (Luke xvii. 20). Religious truth is not reached by "quick turns of self-applauding intellect," nor by demonstrations. It comes another way. The quiet familiarity with the deep true things of life, till on a sudden they are transfigured in the light of God, and truth is a new and glowing thing, independent of arguments and the strange evidence of thaumaturgy—this is the normal way; and Jesus holds by it. The great people, men of law and learning, want more; they want something to substantiate God's messages from without. If Jesus comes to them with a word from God, can he not prove its authenticity preferably with "a sign from the sky" (Mark viii. 11)? For the signs he gives, and the evidence he suggests, are unsatisfactory. "And he sighed deeply in his spirit, and saith, 'Why doth this generation seek after a sign? Verily I say unto you, there shall no sign be given unto this generation.' So he left them and went up into the ship again and went away." That scene is drawn from life.

But why no sign? In the parallel passage we read: " 'The wicked generation and adulterous seeketh a sign, but there shall no sign be given it, but the sign of the prophet Jonah'; so he left them and departed" (Matt. xvi. 4). The real explanation of this reference to Jonah is given by Luke (xi. 32), and missed or misdeveloped in Matthew (Matt. xii. 40). Nineveh recognized instinctively the inherent truth of Jonah's message, and repented. Truth is its own evidence—like leaven in the meal, like seed in the field, it does its work, and its life reveals it. God is known that way. When the chief priests demand of Jesus to be told plainly what is his authority (Mark xi. 27), he carries the matter a stage further: Was the baptism of John, he asks, from heaven, *i.e.* from God, or was it of men? Does God make His message clear, does He properly authenticate Himself?

And the uneasy weighing of alternatives, summarized by the evangelist, leads to the answer that they could not tell whence it was; and Jesus rejoins that he has nothing to say to them about *his* authority. He had taken what we might call an easy cas —where it was evident that God had spoken; and this was all they made of it—they "could not tell." It was plain, then, *either* that these men did not recognize the obvious message of God ("the word of God came upon John," Luke iii. 2), *or* that, if they did recognize it, they thought it did not matter. For the insincere and the trivial there is no message from God, no truth of God—how should there be?

If we pursue this line of thought, we can see how, in Jesus' opinion, a man may be sure of God and of God's word for him. If a man be candid with himself, if he face the common facts of life with seriousness and in the doing of duty, perplexities vanish. Such a man is prepared for the Great Fact, by faithfulness to the little facts, and then God dawns on him in them. This is put directly in the Fourth Gospel (vii. 17), and in parable in the Synoptists. The leaven works, till the whole is leavened; the uneasy process is over and the result achieved. Or, it comes more quietly still—the seed grows while the farmer sleeps and rises, night and day; the blade springs up and the ear forms on the blade, the seed grows in the ear; and the end is reached and God's Kingdom is a reality. Or, the knowledge of God comes like a lightning flash—sudden, illuminative, decisive. "The Son reveals" God to the simple, Jesus said (Matt. xi. 27). The Son of Man may be a disputable figure—"Whosoever speaketh a word against the Son of Man, it shall be forgiven him" (Matt. xii. 32)—but there is no forgiveness in this world, or in any possible real world where God counts at all, for the refusal of the spirit of Truth. So he taught, and all history shows he was right—the refusal of truth is fatal. "Jesus," wrote Matthew Arnold, "never touches *theory*, but bases himself invariably upon experience." It is to experience that Jesus goes to authenticate his message. The real facts of life lead you to God, as the red sky, and the south wind, teach you to foretell the weather (Matt. xvi. 2; Luke xii. 55).

"Eyes and ears," said the Greek thinker, Heraclitus, long before, "are bad witnesses for such as have barbarian souls." The Pharisees discredited Jesus—he "cast out devils by Beelzebub." Did he, he asked, or was it "by the finger of God" (Luke xi. 20)? Is there no evidence of God in restored sanity? But the strength of his position lies in the good news for the poor (Matt. xi. 5), for those who labor and are heavy-laden (Matt. xi. 28)—news of rest and refreshment—as if the intuition of God, with the peace it brings, were its own proof. Truth is reached less by ingenuity than by intensity. To the simple mind, to the true heart, to the pure soul (Matt. v. 8), to those whose gift is peace, Truth comes flooding in—new light on old fact, and new light from old fact—and God is evident. So Jesus judged; and here again, before we decide for or against his view, we have to make sure that we know his meaning, and realize the experience by which he reached his thought. And then, perhaps, God will be more evident to us in our turn. "The Kingdom of God cometh not with observation" (Luke xvii. 20)—it is "within" (Luke xvii. 21); so quietly it comes, that we may not guess how in any particular instance the realization of God came to a soul; but if we are candid and truth-loving we can know it when it has come to ourselves, and we can recognize it when it comes to another. We can recognize it in its power and peace, we can see the greatness of the new knowledge in the new man it makes, in the new life, the man of the great spirit, of the great action, the man of the great quiet, the man who has the peace of God.

What does the discovery of God mean? Jesus himself speaks of a man turning right about, being converted (Matt. xviii. 3); of the revision of all ideas, of all standards, of all values. He gives us two beautiful pictures to illustrate what it means; and it repays us to linger over them. First, there is the Treasure Finder. He is in the country, digging perhaps in another man's field, or idling in the open; and by accident he stumbles on a buried treasure. Palestine was like Belgium—a land with a long history of wars fought on its soil by foreigners, Babylon or Assyria against Egypt, Ptolemies against Seleucids. It was the only available route for attack either on Egypt by land, or on Syria or Mesopotamia or Babylon from the Southern Mediterranean. In such a land when the foreign army marched through, a man had best hide his treasure and hope to find it again in better times, and again and again the secret of its place of burial died with him. The Treasure Finder had no lord of the manor to think of, no Treasury department. He made a great discovery, and made it initially for himself, and his own—"and for joy thereof he goeth and selleth all that he hath and buyeth that field." We can see him full of his discovery, full of eagerness and trying to hide his inner joy, as he realizes every penny he can manage, and achieves the great transaction which gives him the field and the treasure. The salient points are a sudden and great joy, an instant resolution, a complete sacrifice of everything, and a life unexpectedly and infinitely enriched. And so it is, says Jesus, with the Kingdom of God (Matt. xiii. 44).

The Pearl Merchant is a more interesting figure. Perhaps we may picture him middle-aged, a trifle worn, somewhat silent, a man of keen eyes. He has been in his trade for years, and he is a master at it. By now he has a knowledge which years give to a man in earnest—a knowledge more like instinct than anything acquired. A glance at pearls on a table—this, and this, and this he will take—the other, perhaps; he would look at that one—the rest? he shook his head and did not look at them—he saw without looking. One day he is told of a pearl—a good one. He is not surprised, for pearls are always good when they are offered for sale. But again a glance is enough. The price? Yes, it is high, but he will take the pearl, but he must be allowed till evening to get the money. He goes away and sells his stock—the little collection of pearls in his wallet, representing "the experience of a life-time," all of them good, as he very well knows; and he sells them for what he can get—at a loss, if it must be. Yesterday's bargainer cuts down his price for this and that pearl, and he is taken up; he never expected to do so well against the old dealer, and he laughs. But the merchant is content, too; he has sold all his pearls for what they would fetch—lost money on them, yes, and been laughed at behind his back. But he owns the one pearl of great price; it is his, and he is satisfied. There is no reference to joy here or exultation; but there is the same instant recognition of the opportunity, the same resolve, the same sacrifice, and the same great acquisition (Matt. xiii. 45).

Both parables begin with a reference to the Kingdom of God—to that Rule and Kingship of God, the knowledge of which makes all the difference to a man. A small grammatical difference points us beyond minutiæ to the common experience of the two men. Each makes a great discovery, and takes action in a great and urgent resolve; and they are both repaid. If we are to understand the two parables in the sense intended by Jesus, the term "God" must become alive to us with all the life and power and love that the name implies for him. Then to grasp that this Father of Jesus is King—that the God of his thoughts, of his faith, with all the tenderness and the power combined that Jesus teaches us to see in Him—rules the universe, controls our destiny and loves us—this is the experience that Jesus compares with that of the Treasure Finder and the Pearl Merchant—worth, he suggests, everything a man has, and more than all.

In passing, we may notice that these stories suggest that this experience may be reached in different ways. In the parables of the seed and the leaven he indicates a natural, quiet and unconscious growth, a story without crisis, though full of change. To the Treasure Finder the discovery is a surprise—how came Jesus so far into the minds of men as to know what a surprise God can be, and how joyful a surprise? The Pearl Merchant, on the other hand, has lived in the region where he makes his discovery. He is the type that lives and moves in the atmosphere of high and true thought, that knows whatsoever things are pure and lovely and of good report, of help and use; he is no stranger to great and inspiring ideas. And one day, in no strange way, by no accident, but in the ordinary round of life, he comes on something that transcends all he has been seeking, all he has known —the One thing worth all. There is little surprise about it, no wild elation, but nothing is allowed to stand in the way of an instant entrance into the great experience— and the great experience is, Jesus says, God.

To see God, to know God—that is what Jesus means —to get away from "all the fuss and trouble" of life into the presence of God, to know he is ours, to see him smile, to realize that he wants us to stay there, that he is a real Father with a father's heart, that his love is on the same wonderful scale as every one of his attributes, and in reality far more intelligible than any of them. That is the picture Jesus draws. The sheer incredible love of God, the wonderful change it means for all life—that is his teaching, and he encourages us, in the words of the Shorter Catechism, "to enjoy God for ever," as Jesus himself does. Those who learn his secret enjoy God in reality. Wherever they see God with the eyes of Jesus, it is joy and peace. And they realize with deepening emotion that this also is God's gift, as Jesus said (Luke viii. 10; xii. 32).

Jesus entirely recast mankind's common ideas of holiness. It is no longer asceticism, no longer the mystical trance, no longer the "fussiness," with which the early Christian reproached the Jew, which still haunts all the religions of taboo and merit, and even Christianity in some forms. Where men think of holiness as freedom from sin, the negative conception reacts on life. They begin at the wrong end. Solomon Schechter, the great Jewish scholar, once said of Oxford, that "they practice fastidiousness there, and call it holiness." Unfortunately Oxford has no monopoly of that type of holiness. But with Jesus holiness is a much simpler and more natural thing—as natural as the happy, easy life of father and child, and it rests on mutual faith. It is Theocentric, positive, active rather than passive—not a state, but a relation and a force. Holiness with him is a living relation with the living God. That is why the first feature in it that strikes us is Courage. "Be of good cheer; be not afraid"; that note rings through the Gospels, and how much it means, and has meant, in sweet temper and cheerfulness in the very chequered history of the Church! His is the great voice of Hope in the world. "The Lord Jesus Christ, who is our Hope," Paul said (1 Tim. i. 1). Even on the Cross, according to one text, Jesus said to the penitent thief: "Courage! To-day thou shalt be with me in paradise" (Luke xxiii. 43). We may not know where or what paradise is, but the rest is intelligible and splendid: "Courage; to-day thou shalt be with me." Look at the brave hearts the Gospel has made in every age; how venturesome they are! and we find the same venturesomeness in Jesus—for instance, as a German scholar emphasizes, in that episode of the daughter of Jairus. The messenger comes and says she is dead. Anybody else would stop, but Jesus goes on. That is a great piece of interpretation. Look again at his venturesomeness in trusting the Gospel to the twelve—and to us—and in facing the Cross. "It was his knowledge of God," says Professor Peabody, "that gave him his tranquillity of mind."[1]

---

[1] Peabody, *Jesus Christ and Christian Character*, p. 97.

"Jesus," says Dr. Cairns, "said that no one ever trusted God enough, and that was the source of all the sin and tragedy." Look at his emphasis again and again on faith; and the language is not that of guesswork; they are the words of the great Son of Fact, who based himself on experience. "Have faith in God" (Mark xi. 22). "Be not afraid, only believe" (Mark v. 36). "All things are possible to him that believeth" (Mark ix. 23). When he criticizes his disciples, it is on the score of their want of faith—"O ye of little faith"—it has been taken as almost a nickname for them. In the hour of trial and danger they may trust to "the Spirit of your Father" (Matt. x. 20). It is remarkable what value he attaches to faith even of the slightest—"faith as a grain of mustard seed" (Matt. xvii. 20)—it is little, but it is of the seed order, a living thing of the most immense vitality with the promise of growth and usefulness in it.

This brings us to the question of Prayer. Some of us, of course, do not believe very much in prayer for certain philosophical reasons, which perhaps, as a matter of fact, are not quite as sound as we think, because our definition of prayer is a wrong one, resting on insufficient experience and insufficient reflection. What is prayer?

We shall agree that it is the act by which man definitely tries to relate his soul and life to God. What Jesus then teaches on prayer will illuminate what he means by God; and conversely his conception of God will throw new light upon the whole problem of prayer. It is plain history that Jesus, the great Son of Fact, believed in prayer, told men to pray, and prayed himself. The Gospels and the Epistle to the Hebrews lay emphasis on his practice. Early in the morning he withdrew to the desert (Mark

i. 35), late at night he remained on the hillside for prayer (Mark vi. 46). Wearied by the crowds that thronged him, he kept apart and continued in prayer. He prays before he chooses the disciples (Luke vi. 12). He gives thanks to God on the return of the seventy from their missionary journey (Luke x. 21). Prayer is associated with the confession of Cæsarea Philippi (Luke ix. 18), with the Mount of Transfiguration (Luke ix. 29), with Gethsemane (Luke xxii. 41). The writer to the Hebrews speaks of his "strong crying and tears" (Heb. v. 7) in prayer. The Gospels even mention what we should call his unanswered prayers. The prayer before the calling of the Twelve does not exclude Judas; and the cup does not pass in spite of the prayer in Gethsemane. It is as if we had something to learn from the unanswered prayers of our Master. Certainly the content of the Gospel for us would have been poorer if they had been answered in our sense of the word; and this fact, taken with his own teaching on prayer, and his own submission to the Father's will, may help us over some of our difficulties. But Jesus had no doubt or fear about prayer being answered. "Ask, and it shall be given you; seek, and ye shall find; knock, and it shall be opened unto you" (Luke xi. 9)—are not ambiguous statements in the least; and they come from one "who based himself on experience." It is worth thinking out that the experience of Jesus lies behind his recommendation of prayer. All his clear-eyed knowledge of God speaks in these plain sentences.

"As he was praying, they ask him, Teach us to pray, as John also taught his disciples" (Luke xi. 1). It looks as if at times his disciples caught him at prayer or even overheard him, and felt that here was prayer that took them out beyond all they had ever known of prayer. There were men whom John had taught to pray; was it they who asked Jesus to teach them over again? There may have been some of them who had learnt the Pharisee's way in prayer, and some who stuck to the simpler way they had been taught in childhood. In each case the old ways were outgrown.

We can put together what he taught them. In the first place, the thing must be real and individual—the first requirement always with Jesus. The public prayer of ostentation is out of the reckoning; it is nothing. Jesus chooses the quiet and solitary place for his intercourse with his Father. The real prayer is to the Father in secret—His affair. And it will be earnest beyond what most of us think. We are so familiar with Gospel and parable that we do not take in the strenuousness of Jesus' way in prayer. The importunate widow (Luke xviii. 2) and the friend at midnight (Luke xi. 5) are his types of insistent and incessant earnestness. Do you, he asks, pray with anything like their determination to be heard? The knock at the door and the pleading voice continue till the request is granted—in each case by a reluctant giver. But God is not reluctant, Jesus says, though God, too, will choose his own time to answer (Luke xviii. 7). It does not mean the mechanical reiteration of the heathen (Matt. vi. 7)—not at all, that is not the business of praying; but the steady earnest concentration on the purpose, with the deeper and deeper clarification of the thought as we press home into God's presence till we get there. It was so that he prayed, we may be sure. It is not idly that prayer has been called "the greatest task of the Christian man"; it will not be an easy thing, but a strenuous.

One part of the difficulty of prayer is recognized by Jesus over and over again. Men do not really *quite* believe that they will be answered—they are "of little faith." But he tells them with emphasis, in one form of words and another, driving it home into them, that "all things are possible with God" (Mark x. 27)—"have faith in God" (Mark xi. 22). One can imagine how he fixes them with the familiar steady gaze, pauses, and then with the full weight of his personality in his words, and meaning them to give to his words the full value he intends, says: "Have faith in God." To see him and to hear him must have given that faith of itself. If the friend in the house to your knowledge has the loaves, you will knock till you get them; and has not God the gifts for you that you need? Is he short of the power to help, or is it the will to help that is wanting in God?

It all comes back to Jesus' conception of God. Here, as elsewhere, we sacrifice far more than we dream by our lazy way of using his words without making the effort to give them his connotation. To turn again to passages already quoted, will a father give his son a serpent instead of the fish for which he asks, a stone for bread? It is unthinkable; God—will God do less? It all goes back again to the relation of father and child, to the love of God; only into the thought Jesus puts a significance which we have not character or love enough to grasp. "Your Father knoweth that ye have need of these things," he says about the matters that weigh heaviest with us (Luke xii. 30). Even if we suppose Luke's reference to the Father giving the Holy Spirit to those who ask (Luke xi. 13), to owe something to the editor's hand—it was an editor with some Christian experience—it is clear that

Jesus steadily implies that the heavenly Father has better things than food and clothing for his children. How much of a human father is available for his children? Then will not the heavenly Father, Jesus suggests, give on a larger scale, and give Himself; in short, be available for the least significant of His own children in all His fulness and all His Fatherhood? And even if they do not ask, because they do not know their need, will he not answer the prayers that others, who do know, make for them? Jesus at all events made a practice of intercession—"I prayed for thee," he said to Peter (Luke xxii. 32)—and the writers of the New Testament feel that it is only natural for Jesus, Risen, Ascended, and Glorified, to make intercession for us still (Rom. viii. 34; Heb. vii. 25).

We have again to think out what God's Fatherhood implies and carries with it for Jesus.

"The recurrence of the sweet and deep name, Father, unveils the secret of his being. His heart is at rest in God."[1] Rest in God is the very note of all his being, of all his teaching—the keynote of all prayer in his thought. "Our Father, who art in heaven," our prayers are to begin—and perhaps they are not to go on till we realize what we are saying in that great form of speech. It is certain that as these words grow for us into the full stature of their meaning for Jesus, we shall understand in a more intimate way what the whole Gospel is in reality.

The writer to the Hebrews has here an interesting suggestion for us. Using the symbolism of the Hebrew religion and its tabernacle, he compares Jesus to the

[1] H. R. Mackintosh, *The Doctrine of the Person of Jesus Christ*, p. 399.

High Priest, but Jesus, he says, does not enter into the holiest alone. "Having therefore, brethren, boldness to enter into the holiest by the blood of Jesus, by a new and living way, which he hath consecrated for us . . . let us draw near with a true heart in full assurance of faith" (Heb. x. 19). In the previous chapter he discards the symbol and "speaks things"—"Christ is not entered into the holy places made with hands, which are the figures of the true; but into heaven itself, now to appear in the presence of God for us" (Heb. ix. 24). There he touches what has been the faith of the Church throughout—that in Christ we reach the presence of God. Without saying so much in so many words, Jesus implies this in all his attitude to prayer. God is there, and God loves you, and loves to have you speak with him. No one has ever believed this very much outside the radius of Christ's person and influence. It is, when we give the words full weight, an essentially Christian faith, and it depends on our relation to Jesus Christ.

Jesus was quite explicit with his friends in telling them they did not know what to ask, but he showed them himself what they should ask. "Seek ye first the kingdom of God and his righteousness" (Matt. vi. 33), he says, and tells us to pray for the forgiveness of our sins and for deliverance from evil. Pray, too, "Thy kingdom come." "Pray ye the Lord of the harvest, that he will send forth laborers into his harvest" (Matt. ix. 38). This is perhaps the only place where he asked his disciples to pray for his great work. Identification with God's purposes—identification with the individual needs of those we love and those we ought to love—identification with the world's sin and misery—these seem to be his canons of prayer for us, as for himself. For both in what he teaches others and in what he does himself, he makes it a definite prerequisite of all prayer that we say: "Thy will be done." Prayer is essentially dedication, deeper and fuller as we use it more and come more into the presence of God. Obedience goes with it; "we must cease to pray or cease to disobey," one or the other. If we are half-surrendered, we are not very bright about our prayers, because we do not quite believe that God will really look after the things about which we are anxious. We must indeed go back to what Jesus said about God; we had better even leave off praying for a moment till we see what he says, and then begin again with a clearer mind.

"Ask, and ye shall receive," he says; and if we have no obedience, or love, or faith, or any of the great things that make prayer possible, he suggests that we can ask for them and have them. The Gospel gives us an illustration in the man who prayed: "Lord, I believe; help thou mine unbelief" (Mark ix. 24). But it is plain we have to understand that we are asking for great things, and it is to them rather than to the obvious little things that Jesus directs our thoughts. Not away from the little things, for if God is a real Father he will wish to have his children talk them over with him—"little things please little minds," yes, and great minds when the little minds are dear to them—but not little things all the time. There is a variant to the saying about seeking first the Kingdom of Heaven, which Clement of Alexandria preserves. Perhaps it is a mere slip, but God, it has been said, can use misquotations; and Clement's quotation, or misquotation, certainly represents the thought of Jesus, and it may give us a hint for our own practice: "Ask," saith he, "the great things, and the little things will be added unto you."

The object of Jesus was to induce men to base all life on God. Short-range thinking, like the rich fool's, may lead to our forgetting God; but Jesus incessantly lays the emphasis on the thought-out life; and that, in the long run, means a new reckoning with God. That is what Jesus urges—that we should think life out, that we should come face to face with God and see him for what he is, and accept him. He means us to live a life utterly and absolutely based on God—life on God's lines of peace-making and ministry, the "denial of self," a complete forgetfulness of self in surrender to God, obedience to God, faith in God, and the acceptance of the sunshine of God's Fatherhood. He means us to go about things in God's way—forgiving our enemies, cherishing kind thoughts about those who hate us or despise us or use us badly (Matt. v. 44), praying for them. This takes us right back into the common world, where we have to live in any case; and it is there that he means us to live with God—not in trance, but at work, in the family, in business, shop, and street, doing all the little things and all the great things that God wants us to do, and glad to do them just because we are his children and he is our Father. Above all, he would have us "think like God" (Mark viii. 33); and to reach this habit of "thinking like God," we have to live in the atmosphere of Jesus, "with him" (Mark iii. 14). All this new life he made possible for us by being what he was—once again a challenge to re-explore Jesus. "The way to faith in God and to love for man," said Dr. Cairns at Mohonk, "is as of old to come nearer to the living Jesus."

CHAPTER VI

JESUS AND MAN

WHEN, on his last journey, Jesus came in sight of Jerusalem, Luke tells us that he wept (Luke xix. 41). There is an obvious explanation of this in the extreme tension under which he was living—everything turned upon the next few days, and everything would be decided at Jerusalem; but while he must have felt this, it cannot have been the cause of his weeping. Nor should we look for it altogether in the appeal which a great city makes to emotion.

> Dull would he be of soul who could pass by
> A sight so touching in its majesty.

Yet it was not the architecture that so deeply moved Jesus; the temple, which was full in view, was comparatively new and foreign. There is little suggestion in the Gospels that Art meant anything to him, perhaps it meant little to the writers. As for the temple, he found it "a den of thieves" (Luke xix. 46); and he prophesied that it would be demolished, and of all its splendid buildings, its goodly stones and votive offerings, which so much impressed his disciples, not one stone would be left upon another stone (Mark xiii. 2; Luke xxi. 5). But the traditions of Jerusalem wakened thoughts in him of the story of his people, thoughts with a tragic color. Jerusalem was the place where prophets were killed (Luke

xiii. 34), the scene and center, at once, of Israel's deepest emotions, highest hopes, and most awful failures. "O Jerusalem! Jerusalem!" he had said in sadness as he thought of Israel's holy city, "which killest the prophets and stonest them that are sent unto thee, how often would I have gathered thy children together, as a hen doth gather her brood under her wings, and ye would not!" (Luke xiii. 34).

And now he is in sight of Jerusalem. The city and the temple suddenly meet his view, as he reaches the height, and he is deeply moved. Any reflective mind might well have been stirred by the thought of the masses of men gathered there. Nothing is so futile as an arithmetical numbering of people, for after a certain point figures paralyze the imagination, and after that they tell the mind little or nothing. But here was actually assembled the Jewish people, coming in swarms from all the world, for the feast; here was Judaism at its most pious; here was the pilgrim center with all it meant of aspiration and blindness, of simple folly and gross sin. The sight of the city—the doomed city, as he foresaw—the thought of his people, their zeal for God and their alienation from God—it all comes over him at once, and, with a sudden rush of feeling, he apostrophizes Jerusalem—"If thou hadst known, even thou, at least in this thy day, the things which belong unto thy peace! But now they are hid from thine eyes. . . . Thou knewest not the time of thy visitation!" (Luke xix. 42-44).

It is quite plain from the Gospels that crowds had always an appeal for Jesus. At times he avoided them; but when they came about him, they claimed him and possessed him. Over and over again, we read of his pity for them—"he saw a great multitude and was moved with compassion toward them" (Matt. xiv. 14)—of his thought for their weariness and hunger, his reflection that they might "faint by the way" on their long homeward journeys (Mark viii. 3), and his solicitude about their food. Whatever modern criticism makes of the story of his feeding multitudes, it remains that he was markedly sensitive to the idea of hunger. Jairus is reminded that his little girl will be the better for food (Mark v. 43). The rich are urged to make feasts for the poor, the maimed and the blind (Luke xiv. 12). The owner of the vineyard, in the parable, pays a day's wage for an hour's work, when an hour was all the chance that the unemployed laborer could find (Matt. xx. 9). No sanctity could condone for the devouring of widows' houses (Matt. xxiii. 14).

The great hungry multitudes haunt his mind. The story of the rich young ruler shows this (Mark x. 17-22). Here was a man of birth and education, whose face and whose speech told of a good heart and conscience—a man of charm, of the impulsive type that appealed to Jesus. Jesus "looked on him," we read. The words recall Plato's picture of Socrates looking at the jailer, how "he looked up at him in his peculiar way, like a bull" —the old man's prominent eyes were fixed on the fellow, glaring through the brows above them, and Socrates' friends saw them and remembered them when they thought of the scene. As Jesus' eyes rested steadily on this young man, the disciples saw in them an expression they knew —"Jesus, looking on him, loved him." Their talk was of eternal life; and, no doubt to his surprise, Jesus asked the youth if he had kept the commandments; how did he stand as regarded murder, theft, adultery? The steady gaze followed the youth's impetuous answer, and then came the recommendation to sell all that he had and give to the poor—"and, Come! Follow me!" At this, we read in a fragment of the *Gospel according to the Hebrews* (preserved by Origen), "the rich man began to scratch his head, and it did not please him. And the Lord said to him, 'How sayest thou, "The law I have kept and the prophets?" For it is written in the law, "thou shalt love thy neighbor as thyself"; and behold! many who are thy brethren, sons of Abraham, are clad in filth and dying of hunger, and thy house is full of many good things, and nothing at all goes out from it to them.' And he turned and said to Simon, his disciple, who was sitting beside him: 'Simon, son of John, it is easier for a camel to go through a needle's eye than for a rich man to enter into the Kingdom of Heaven.' " We need not altogether reject this variant of the story.

But it was more than the physical needs of the multitude that appealed to Jesus. "Man's Unhappiness, as I construe," says Teufelsdröckh in *Sartor Resartus,* "comes of his Greatness, it is because there is an Infinite in him, which with all his cunning he cannot quite bury under the Finite. Will the whole Finance Ministers and Upholsterers and Confectioners of modern Europe undertake, in joint-stock company, to make one Shoeblack happy?" We read in a passage, which it is true, is largely symbolic, that one of Jesus' quotations from the Old Testament was that "Man shall not live by bread alone" (Luke iv. 4). Hunger is a real thing—horribly real; but it is comparatively easy to deal with, and man has deeper needs. The Shoeblack, according to Teufelsdröckh, wants

"God's infinite universe altogether to himself"—in the simpler words of Jesus, he is never happy till he says, "I will arise and go to my Father" (Luke xv. 18).

This craving for the Father the men of Jesus' day tried to fill with the law; and, when the law failed to satisfy it, they had nothing further to suggest, except their fixed idea that "God heareth not sinners" (John ix. 31). They despaired of the great masses and left them alone. They did not realize, as Jesus did, that the Father also craves for his children. When Jesus saw the simpler folk thus forsaken, the picture rose in his mind of sheep, worried by dogs or wolves, till they fell, worn out—sheep without a shepherd (Matt. ix. 36). Every one remembers the shepherd of the parable who sought the one lost sheep until he found it, and how he brought it home on his shoulders (Luke xv. 5). But there is another parable, we might almost say, of ninety and nine lost sheep—a parable, not developed, but implied in the passage of Matthew, and it is as significant as the other, for our Good Shepherd[1] has to ask his friends to help him in this case. The appeal that lay in the sheer misery and helplessness of masses of men was one of the foundations of the Christian Church.

It is worth noticing that Jesus stands alone in refusing to despair of the greater part of mankind. Contempt was in his eyes the unpardonable sin (Matt. v. 22). How swift and decisive is his anger with those who make others stumble! (Luke xvii. 2). The parable of the lost sheep

---

[1] The Good Shepherd, by the way, is a phrase from the Fourth Gospel (John x. 11), but we think most often of the Good Shepherd as carrying the sheep, and that comes from Luke, and is in all likelihood nearer the parable of Jesus.

reveals what he held to be God's feeling for the hopeless man; and, as we have seen, his constant aim is to lead men to "think like God." The lost soul matters to God. He sums up his own work in the world in much the same language as he uses about the shepherd in the parable: "The Son of Man is come to seek and to save that which is lost" (Luke xix. 10). The taunt that he was the "friend of publicans and sinners" really described what he was and wished to be (Luke vii. 34). God was their Heavenly Father. The sight, then, of the masses of his countrymen, like worried sheep, worn, scattered, lost, and hopeless, waked in him no shade of doubt—on the contrary, it was further proof to him of the soundness of his message. Changing his simile, he told his disciples that the harvest was great, but the laborers few, and he asked them to pray the Lord of the harvest to thrust forth laborers into His harvest (Matt. ix. 38). The very name "Lord of the harvest" implies faith in God's competence and understanding. From the first, he seems to have held up before his followers that this wide service was to be their work—"Come ye after me," he said, "and I will make you to become fishers of men" (Mark i. 17)—men, who should really "catch men" (Luke v. 10).

Like all for whom the world has had a meaning, Jesus, as we have seen, accepted the necessary conditions of man's life. Human misery and need were widespread, but God's Fatherhood was of compass fully as wide, and Jesus relied upon it. "Your heavenly Father knows," he said (Matt. vi. 32), and "with God all things are possible" (Mark x. 27). The very miseries of the oppressed and hopeless people added grounds to his confidence. People who had touched bottom in sounding the human spirit's capacity for misery, were for him the "ripe harvest" (Matt. ix. 37), only needing to be gathered (Mark iv. 29). He understood them, and he knew that he had the healing for all their troubles. With full assurance of the truth of his words, he cried: "Come unto me all ye that labor and are heavy laden, and I will give you rest" (Matt. xi. 28). He spoke of a rest which careless familiarity obscures for us. What understanding and sympathy he shows, when he adds: "My yoke is easy, and my burden is light!" Misery, poverty and hunger, he had found, taught men to see realities. The hungry, at least, were not likely to mistake a stone for bread—they had a ready test for it, on which they could rely. Poverty threw open the road to the Kingdom of God. The clearing away of all temporary satisfactions, of all that cloaked the soul's deepest needs, prepared men for real relations with the greatest Reality—with God. So that Jesus boldly said: "Blessed are ye poor"; "Blessed are ye that hunger now"; "Blessed are ye that weep now" (Luke vi. 20, 21); but he had no idea that they were always to weep. If it was his to care for men's hunger, it was not likely that he would have no comfort for their tears—"Ye shall find rest unto your souls" (Matt. xi. 29)—"They shall be comforted" (Matt. v. 4).

It was in large part upon the happiness which he was to bring to the poor that Jesus based his claim to be heard. There is little reasonable ground for doubt that he healed diseases. Of course we cannot definitely pronounce upon any individual case reported; the diagnosis might be too hasty, and the trouble other than was supposed; but it is well known that such healings do occur—and that they occurred in Jesus' ministry, we can well believe. So when he was challenged as to his credentials, he pointed to misery relieved; and the culmination of everything, the crowning feature of his work, he found in his "good news for the poor." The phrase he borrowed from Isaiah (lxi. 1), but he made it his own—the splendid promises in Isaiah for "the poor, the broken-hearted, captives, blind and bruised," appealed to him. Time has laid its hand upon his word, and dulled its freshness. "Gospel" and "evangelical" are no longer words of sheer happiness like Jesus' "good news"—they are technical terms, used in handbooks and in controversy; while for Jesus the "good news for the poor" was a new word of delight and inspiration.

The center in all the thoughts of Jesus, as we have to remind ourselves again and again, is God. If, as Dr. D. S. Cairns puts it, "Jesus Christ is the great believer in man," it is—if we are reading him aright at all—because God believes in man. Let us remind ourselves often of that. "Thou hast made us for Thyself," said Augustine in the famous sentence, of which we are apt to emphasize the latter half, "and our heart knows no rest till it rests in Thee" (*Confessions*, i. 1). Jesus would have us emphasize the former clause as well, and believe it. The keynote of his whole story is God's love; the Father is a real father—strange that one should have to write the small *f* to get the meaning! All that Jesus has taught us of God, we must bring to bear on man. For it is hard to believe in man—"What is man that thou shouldest magnify him? and that thou shouldest set thine heart upon him?" quotes the author of *Job* in a great ironical passage (Job vii. 17; from Psalm viii. 4). The elements and the stars come over us, as they came over

George Fox in the Vale of Beavor;—what *is* man? Can one out of fifteen hundred millions of human beings living on one planet matter to God, when there are so many planets and stars, and there have been so many generations? Can he matter? It all depends on how we conceive of God. Here it is essential to give all the meaning to the term "God" that Jesus gave to it, to believe in God as Jesus believed in God, if we are to understand the fulness of Jesus' "good news." It all depends on God—on whether Jesus was right about God; and after all on Jesus himself. "A thing of price is man," wrote Synesius about 410 A. D., 'because for him Christ died." The two things go together—Jesus' death and Jesus' Theocentric thought of man.

It is a familiar criticism of idealists and other young hearts, that it is easy to idealize what one does not know. *Omne ignotum pro magnifico* is the old epigram of Tacitus. It is not every believer in man, nor every "Friend of man," who knows men as Jesus did. Like Burns and Carlyle and others who have interpreted man to us to some purpose, he grew up in the home of laboring people. He was a working man himself, a carpenter. He must have learnt his carpentry exactly as every boy learns it, by hammering his fingers instead of the nail, sawing his own skin instead of the wood—and *not* doing it again. He knew what it was to have an aching back and sweat on the face; how hard money is to earn, and how quickly it goes. He makes it clear that money is a temptation to men, and a great danger; but he never joins the moralists and cranks in denouncing it. He always talks sense —if the expression is not too lowly to apply to him. He sees what can be done with money, what a tool it can be in a wise man's hands—how he can make friends "by means of the mammon of unrighteousness" (Luke xvi. 9), for example, by giving unexpectedly generous wages to men who missed their chances (Matt. xx. 15), by feeding Lazarus at the gate, and perhaps by having his sores properly attended to (Luke xvi. 20). That he understood how pitifully the loss of a coin may affect a household of working people, one of his most beautiful parables bears witness (Luke xv. 8-10). With work he had no quarrel. He draws many of his parables from labor, and he implies throughout that it is the natural and right thing for man. To be holy in his sense, a man need not leave his work. Clement of Alexandria, in his famous saying about the ploughman continuing to plough, and knowing God as he ploughs, and the seafaring man, sticking to his ship and calling on the heavenly pilot as he sails, is in the vein of Jesus.[1] There were those whom he called to leave all, to distribute their wealth, and to follow him; but he chose them (Mark iii. 13, 14); it was not his one command for all men (*cf.* Mark v. 19). But, as we shall shortly see, it is implied by his judgments of men that he believed in work and liked men who "put their backs into it"—their backs, eyes, and their brains too.

Pain, the constant problem of man, and perhaps more, of woman—of unmarried woman more especially—he never discussed as modern people discuss it. He never made light of pain any more than of poverty; he understood physical as well as moral distress. Nor did he, like some of his contemporaries and some modern people, exaggerate the place of pain in human experience.

---

[1] Clement, *Protrepticus*, 100, 3, 4.

He shared pain, he sympathized with suffering; and his understanding of pain, and, above all, his choice of pain, taught men to reconsider it and to understand it, and altered the attitude of the world toward it. His tenderness for the suffering of others taught mankind a new sympathy, and the *nosokomeion*, the hospital for the sick, was one of the first of Christian institutions to rise, when persecution stopped and Christians could build. "And the blind and the lame came to him in the temple, and he healed them," says Matthew (xxi. 14) in a memorable phrase. I have heard it suggested that it was irregular for them to come into the temple courts; but they gravitated naturally to Jesus.

The mystic is never quite at leisure for other people's feelings and sufferings; he is essentially an individualist; he must have his own intercourse with God, and other people's affairs are apt to be an interruption, an impertinence. "I have not been thinking of the community; I have been thinking of Christ," said a Bengali to me, who was wavering between the Brahmo Samaj and Christianity. The blessed Angela of Foligno was rather glad to be relieved of her husband and children, who died and left her leisure to enjoy the love of God. All this is quite unlike the real spirit of the historical Jesus. "Himself took our infirmities and bare our sicknesses," was a phrase of Isaiah that came instinctively to the minds of his followers (Matt. viii. 17, roughly after Isaiah liii. 4). Perhaps when we begin to understand what is meant by the Incarnation, we may find that omnipotence has a great deal more to do than we have supposed with natural sympathy and the genius for entering into the sorrows and sufferings of other people.

One side of the work of Jesus must never be forgotten. His attitude to woman has altered her position in the world. No one can study society in classical antiquity or in non-Christian lands with any intimacy and not realize this. Widowhood in Hinduism, marriage among Mohammedans—they are proverbs for the misery of women. Even the Jew still prays: "Blessed art thou, O Lord our God! King of the Universe, who hast not made me a woman." The Jewish woman has to be grateful to God, because He "hath made me according to His will"—a thanksgiving with a different note, as the modern Jewess, Amy Levy, emphasized in her brilliant novel, where her heroine, very like herself, corrected her prayerbook to make it more explicit—"cursed art Thou, O Lord our God! Who hast made me a woman." Paul must have known these Jewish prayers, for he emphasized that in Christ there is neither male nor female (Gal. iii. 28). Paul had his views—the familiar old ways of Tarsus inspired them[1]—as to woman's dress and deportment, especially the veil; but he struck the real Christian note here, and laid stress on the fact of what Jesus had done and is doing for women. There is no reference made by Jesus to woman that is not respectful and sympathetic; he never warns men against women. Even the most degraded women find in him an amazing sympathy; for he has the secret of being pure and kind at the same time—his purity has not to be protected; it is itself a purifying force. He draws some of his most delightful parables from woman's work, as we

[1] The more or less contemporary Greek orator, Dio Chrysostom, refers to the old-fashioned ways of the Tarsiots, especially mentioning their insistence on women wearing veils.

have seen. It is recorded how, when he spoke of the coming disaster of Jerusalem, he paused to pity poor pregnant women and mothers with little babies in those bad times (Luke xxi. 23; Matt. xxiv. 19). Critics have remarked on the place of woman in Luke's Gospel, and some have played with fancies as to the feminine sources whence he drew his knowledge—did the women who ministered to Jesus, Joanna, for instance, the wife of Chuza (Luke viii. 3), tell him these illuminative stories of the Master? In any case Jesus' new attitude to woman is in the record; and it has so reshaped the thought of mankind, and made it so hard to imagine anything else, that we do not readily grasp what a revolution he made—here as always by referring men's thoughts back to the standard of God's thoughts, and supporting what he taught by what he was.

Mark has given us one of our most familiar pictures of Jesus sitting with a little child on his knee and "in the crook of his arm." (The Greek participle which gives this in Mark ix. 36 and x. 16 is worth remembering—it is vivid enough.) Mothers brought their children to him, "that he should put his hands on them and pray" (Matt. xix. 13). Matthew (xxi. 15) says that children took part in the Triumphal Entry; and Jesus, clear as he was how little the Hosannas of the grown people meant, seems to have enjoyed the children's part in the strange scene. Classical literature, and Christian literature of those ages, offer no parallel to his interest in children. The beautiful words, "suffer little children to come unto me," are his, and they are characteristic of him (Matt. xix. 14); and he speaks of God's interest in children (Matt. xviii. 14)—once more a reference of everything to God to get it in its true perspective. How Jesus likes children!—for their simplicity (Luke xviii. 17), their intuition, their teachableness, we say. But was it not, perhaps, for far simpler and more natural reasons —just because they *were* children, and little, and delightful? We forget his little brothers and sisters, or we eliminate them for theological purposes.

Jesus lays quite an unexpected emphasis on sheer tenderness—on kindness to neighbor and stranger, the instinctive humanity that helps men, if it be only by the swift offer of a cup of cold water (Matt. x. 42). The Good Samaritan came as a surprise to some of his hearers (Luke x. 30). "It is our religion," said a Hindu to a missionary, to explain why he and other Hindus did not help to rescue a fainting man from the railway tracks, nor even offer water to restore him, when the missionary had hauled him on to the platform unaided. Not so the religion of Jesus—"bear ye one another's burdens, and so fulfil the law of Christ," wrote Paul (Gal. vi. 2)—"pursue hospitality" (Rom. xii. 13; the very word runs through the Epistles of the New Testament). And as we shall see in a later chapter, the Last Judgment itself turns on whether a man has kindly instincts or not. Matthew quotes (xii. 20) to describe Jesus' own tenderness the impressive phrase of Isaiah (xlii. 3), "A bruised reed shall he not break."

If it is urged that such things are natural to man—"do not even the publicans the same?" (Matt. v. 46)—Jesus carries the matter a long way further. "Whosoever shall compel thee to go a mile, go with him twain" (Matt. v. 41). The man who would use such compulsion would be the alien soldier, the hireling of Herod or of Rome; and who would wish to cart him and his goods even one mile? "Go two miles," says Jesus—or, if the Syriac translation preserves the right reading, "Go two *extra*." Why? Well, the soldier is a man after all, and by such unsolicited kindness you may make a friend even of a government official—not always an easy thing to do—at any rate you can help him; God helps him; "be ye therefore perfect, even as your Father which is in heaven is perfect" (Matt. v. 48). Ordinary kindness and tenderness could hardly be urged beyond that point; and yet Jesus goes further still. He would have us *pray* for those that despitefully use us (Matt. v. 44)—and in no Pharisaic way, but with the same instinctive love and friendliness that he always used himself. "Father, forgive them; for they know not what they do" (Luke xxiii. 34). There are religions which inculcate the tolerance of wrong aiming at equanimity of mind or acquisition of merit. But Jesus implies on the contrary that in all this also the Christian *denies* himself, does not seek even in this way to save his own soul, but forgets all about it in the service of others, though he finds by and by, with a start, that he has saved it far more effectually than he could have expected (Mark viii. 35; Matt. xxv. 37, 40). The emphasis falls on our duty of kindness and tenderness to all men and women, because we and they are alike God's children.

With his emphasis on tenderness we may group his teaching on forgiveness. He makes the forgiving spirit an antecedent of prayer—"when ye stand praying, forgive, if ye have aught against any; that your Father also which is in heaven may forgive you your trespasses" (Mark xi. 25). "If thou bring thy gift to the altar, and there rememberest that thy brother hath aught against thee; leave there thy gift before the altar, and go thy way, first be reconciled to thy brother, and then come and offer thy gift" (Matt. v. 23, 24). The parable of the king and his debtor (Matt. xviii. 23), painfully true to human nature, brings out the whole matter of our forgiveneness of one another into the light; we are shown it from God's outlook. The teaching as ever is Theocentric. To Peter, Jesus says that a man should be prepared to forgive his brother to seventy times seven —if anybody can keep count so far (Matt. xviii. 21-35). He sees how quarrels injure life, and alienate a man from God. Hence comes the famous saying: "Resist not evil; but whosoever shall smite thee on thy right cheek, turn to him the other also" (Matt. v. 39). He would have men even avoid criticism of one another (Matt. vii. 1-5). Epigrams are seductive, and there is a fascination in the dissection of character; but there is always a danger that a clever characterization, a witty label, may conclude the matter, that a possible friendship may be lost through the very ingenuity with which the man has been labelled, who might have been a friend. It is not a small matter in Jesus' eyes, he puts his view very strongly (Matt. v. 22); and, as we must always remember, he bases himself on fact. We may lose a great deal more than we think by letting our labels stand between us and his words, by our habit of calling them paradoxes and letting them go at that.

It is worth while to look at the type of character that he admires. Modern painters have often pictured Jesus as something of a dreamer, a longhaired, sleepy, abstract kind of person. What a contrast we find in the energy of the real Jesus—in the straight and powerful language which he uses to men, in the sweep and range of his mind, in the profundity of his insight, the drive and compulsiveness of his thinking, in the venturesomeness of his actions. How many of the parables turn on energy? The real trouble with men, he seems to say, is again and again sheer slackness; they will not put their minds to the thing before them, whether it be thought or action. Thus, for instance, the parable of the talents turns on energetic thinking and decisive action; and these are the things that Jesus admires—in the widow who *will* have justice (Luke xviii. 2)—in the virgins who thought ahead and brought extra oil (Matt. xxv. 4)—in the vigorous man who found the treasure and made sure of it (Matt. xiii. 44)—in the friend at midnight, who hammered, hammered, hammered, till he got his loaves (Luke xi. 8)—in the "violent," who "take the Kingdom of Heaven by force" (Matt. xi. 12; Luke xvi. 16)—in the man who will hack off his hand to enter into life (Mark ix. 43). Even the bad steward he commends, because he definitely put his mind on his situation (Luke xvi. 8). As we shall see later on, indecision is one of the things that in his judgment will keep a man outside the Kingdom of God, that make him unfit for it. The matter deserves more study than we commonly give it. You must have a righteousness, he says, which *exceeds* the righteousness of the Pharisees (Matt. v. 20)—and the Pharisees were professionals in righteousness. His tests of discipleship illumine his ideal of character—Theocentric thinking—negation of self—the thought-out life. He will have his disciples count the cost, reckon their forces, calculate quietly the risks before them—right up to the cross

(Luke xiv. 27-33)—like John Bunyan in Bedford Gaol, where he thought things out to the pillory and thence to the gallows, so that, if it came to the gallows, he should be ready, as he says, to leap off the ladder blindfold into eternity. That is the energy of mind that Jesus asks of men, that he admires in men.

On the other side, he is always against the life of drift, the half-thought-out life. There they were, he says, in the days of Noah, eating and drinking, marrying, dreaming—and the floods came and destroyed them (Luke xvii. 27). So ran the old familiar story, and, says Jesus, it is always true; men will drift and dream for ever, heedless of fact, heedless of God—and then ruin, life gone, the soul lost, the Son of Man come, and "you yourselves thrust out" (Luke xiii. 28, with Matt. xxv. 10-13). It is quite striking with what a variety of impressive pictures Jesus drives home his lesson. There is the person who everlastingly *says* and does not *do* (Matt. xxiii. 3)—who promises to work and does not work (Matt. xxi. 28)—who receives a new idea with enthusiasm, but has not depth enough of nature for it to root itself (Mark iv. 6)—who builds on sand, the "Mr. Anything" of Bunyan's allegory; nor these alone, for Jesus is as plain on the unpunctual (Luke xiii. 25), the easy-going (Luke xii. 47), the sort that compromises, that tries to serve God and Mammon (Matt. vi. 24)—all the practical half-and-half people that take their bills quickly and write fifty, that offer God and man about half what they owe them of thought and character and action, and bid others do the same, and count themselves men of the world for their acuteness (Luke xvi. 1-8). And to do them justice, Jesus commends them; they have taken the exact measure of things "in their generation." Their mistake lies in their equation of the fugitive and the eternal; and it is the final and fatal mistake according to Jesus, and a very common one—forgetfulness of God in fact (Luke xii. 20), a mistake that comes from *not* thinking things out. Jesus will have men think everything out to the very end. "He never says: Come unto me, all ye who are too lazy to think for yourselves" (H. S. Coffin). It is energy of mind that he calls for—either with me or against me. He does not recognize neutrals in his war—"he that is not against us is for us" (Luke ix. 50)—"he that is not with me is against me" (Matt. xii. 30).

Where does a man's *Will* point him? That is the question. "Out of the abundance, the overflow, of the heart, the mouth speaketh" (Matt. xii. 34). What is it that a man *wills*, purity or impurity (Matt. v. 28)? It is the inner energy that makes a man; what he says and does is an overflow from what is within—an overflow, it is true, with a reaction. It is what a man *chooses*, and what he *wills*, that Jesus always emphasizes; "God knoweth your hearts" (Luke xvi. 15). Very well then; does a man choose God? That is the vital issue. Does he choose God without reserve, and in a way that God, knowing his heart, will call a whole-hearted choice?

St. Augustine, in a very interesting passage (*Confessions*, viii. 9, 21), remarks upon the fact that, when the mind commands the body, obedience is instantaneous, but that when it commands itself, it meets with resistance. "The mind commands that the mind shall will—it is one and the same mind, and it does not obey." He finds the reason; the mind does not absolutely and entirely (*ex toto*) will the thing, and so it does not absolutely and entirely command it. "There is nothing strange after all in this," he says, "partly to will, partly not to will; but it is a weakness of the mind that it does not arise in its entirety, uplifted by truth, because it is borne down by habit. Thus there are two *Wills*, because one of them is not complete."

The same thought is to be traced in the teaching of Jesus. It is implied in what he says about prayer. There is a want of faith, a half-heartedness about men's prayers; they pray as Augustine says he himself did: "Give me chastity and continence, but not now" (*Confessions*, viii. 7, 17). That is not what Jesus means by prayer—the utterance of the half-Will. Nor is it this sort of surrender to God that Jesus calls for—no, the question is, how thoroughly is a man going to put himself into God's hands? Does he mean to be God's up to the cross and beyond? Does he enlist absolutely on God's terms without a bargain with God, prepared to accept God's will, whatever it is, whether it squares with his liking or not? (*cf.* Luke xvii. 7-10). Are his own desires finally out of the reckoning? Does he, in fact, *deny*—negate—himself (Mark viii. 34)? Jesus calls for disciples, with questions so penetrating on his lips. What a demand to make of men! What faith, too, in men it shows, that he can ask all this with no hint of diminished seriousness!

Jesus is the great believer in men, as we saw in the choice of his twelve. To that group of disciples he trusts the supremest task men ever had assigned to them. Not many wise, not many mighty Paul found at Corinth (1 Cor. i. 26); and it has always been so.

Is it not still the gist of the Gospel that Jesus believes in the writer and the reader of these lines—trusts them with the propagation of God's Kingdom, incredible commission? Jesus was always at leisure for individuals; this was the natural outcome of his faith in men. What else is the meaning of his readiness to spend himself in giving the utmost spiritual truth—no easy task, as experience shows us—even to a solitary listener? If we accept what he tells us of God, we can believe that the individual is worth all that Jesus did and does for him, but hardly otherwise. His gift of discovering interest in uninteresting people, says Phillips Brooks, was an intellectual habit that he gave to his disciples. We think too much "like men"; he would have us "think like God," and think better of odd units and items of humanity than statesmen and statisticians are apt to do. It has been pointed out lately how fierce he is about the man who puts a stumbling-block in the way of even "a little one"—"better for him that a millstone were hanged about his neck, and he were cast into the sea"; no mere phrase—for when he draws a picture, he sees it; he sees this scene, and "better so—for him too!" is his comment (Mark ix. 42). There was, we may remember, a view current in antiquity that when a man was drowned, his soul perished with his body, though I do not know if the Jews held this opinion. It is not likely that Jesus did. What is God's mind, God's conduct, toward those people whom men think they can afford to despise? "Be ye therefore perfect, even as your Father in heaven is perfect" (Matt. v. 48). And to whom did he say this? To the most ordinary people —to Peter and James and John; for all sorts of people he held up this impossible ideal of a perfection like God's. What a faith in man it implies! "All things are possible to him that believes" (Mark ix. 23). Why should not *you* believe? he says.

His faith in the soul's possibilities is boundless, and in marked contrast with what men think of themselves. A man, for instance, will say that he has done his best; but nine times out of ten it means mere fatigue; he is not going to trouble to do any more. How *can* a man know that he has done his best? The Gospel of Jesus comes with its message of the grace of God, and the power of God, to people who are stupid and middle-aged, who are absolutely settled in life, who are conscious of their limitations, who know they are living in a rut and propose to stick to it for the remainder of their days; and Jesus tells them in effect that he means to give them a new life altogether, that he means to have from them service, perfectly incredible to them. No man, he suggests, need be so inured to the stupidity of middle age but there may be a miraculous change in him. A great many people need re-conversion at forty, however Christian they have been before.

This belief of his in the individual man and in the worth of the individual is the very charter of democracy. The original writings of William Tyndale, who first translated the New Testament from Greek into English, contain the essential ideas of democracy already in 1526—the outcome of familiar study of the Gospel. Jesus himself said of Herod: "Go and tell that fox" (Luke xiii. 32). Herod was a king, but he was not above criticism; and Christians have not failed at times to make the criticism of the great that truth requires.

Jesus had no illusions about men; he sees the weak spots; he recognizes the "whited sepulchre" (Matt. xxiii. 27). He is astonished at the unbelief of men and women (Mark vi. 6). He does not understand why they cannot think (Mark viii. 21), but he notes how they see and yet do not see, hear and do not understand (Matt. xiii. 13). He is impressed by their falsity, even in religion (Matt. xv. 8). He knows perfectly well the evil of which the human heart is capable (Matt. xv. 19). A man who steadily looks forward to being crucified by the people he is trying to help is hardly one of the absent-minded enthusiasts, mis-called idealists. There never was, we feel, one who so thoroughly looked through his friends, who loved them so much and yet without a shade of illusion. This brings us to the subject of the next chapter.

In the meantime let us recall what he makes of the wasted life. "In thinking of the case," said Seeley, "they had forgotten the woman"—a common occurrence with those who deal in "cases." It was once severely said of the Head of a College that "if he would leave off caring for his students' souls and care for *them*, he would do better." Jesus does not forget the man in caring for his soul—he likes *him*. He is "the friend of publicans and sinners" (Luke vii. 34); he eats and drinks with them (Mark ii. 14). Let us remember again that these were taunts and were meant to sting; they were not conventional phrases. See how he can enter into the life of a poor creature. There is the wretched little publican, Zacchæus (Luke xix. 1-10)—a squalid little figure of a man, whom people despised. He was used to contempt—it was the portion of the tax-collector enlisted in Roman service against his own people. Jesus comes and sees him up in the tree; he instantly realizes what is happening and invites himself to the house of Zacchæus as a guest; something passes between them without spoken word. The little man slides down the tree—not a proceeding that makes for dignity; and then, with all his inches, he stands up before the whole town, that knew him so well, in a new moral grandeur that adds cubits to his stature. "Half my goods," he says, "I give to the poor. If I have taken anything from any man by false accusation, he shall have it back fourfold." That man belonged to the despised classes. Jesus came into his life; the man became a new man, a pioneer of Christian generosity. Again, there is the woman with the alabaster box, the mere possession of which stamped her for what she was. It was simply a case of the wasted life. I have long wondered if she meant to give him only some of the ointment. A little of it would have been a great gift. But perhaps the lid of the box jammed, and she realized in a moment that it was to be all or nothing—she drew off her sandal and smashed the box to pieces. However she broke it, and whatever her reasons, Mark's words mean that it was thoroughly and finally shivered (Mark xiv. 3). Something had happened which made this woman the pioneer of the Christian habit of giving all for Jesus. The disciples said they had done so (Matt. xix. 27), but they were looking for thrones in exchange (Mark x. 37); she was not. The thief on the cross himself becomes a pioneer for mankind in the Christian way of prayer. "Jesus, remember me!" he says (Luke xxiii. 42). How is it that Jesus comes into the wasted life and makes it new? "One loving heart sets another on fire."

With all his wide outlook on mankind, his great purpose to capture all men, Jesus is remarkable for his omission to devise machinery or organization for the accomplishment of his ends. The tares are left to grow with the wheat (Matt. xiii. 30)—as if Jesus trusted the wheat a good deal more than we do. Alive as he is to the evil in human nature, he never tries to scare men from it, and he seems to have been very little afraid of it. He believed in the power of good—because, after all, God is "Lord of the Harvest" (Matt. ix. 38). He invents no special methods—a loving heart will hit the method needed in the particular case; the Holy Spirit will teach this as well as other things (Matt. x. 19, 20). How far he even organized his church, or left it to organize itself if it so wished, students may discuss. Would he have trusted even the best organized church as such? Does not what we mean by the Incarnation imply putting everything in the long run on the individual, quickened into new life by a new relation with God and taught a new love of men by Jesus himself? The heart of friendship and the heart of the Incarnation are in essence the same thing—giving oneself in frankness and love to him who will accept, and by them winning him who refuses. Has not this been the secret of the spread of the Gospel? The simplicity of the whole thing, and the power of it, grow upon us as we study them. But after all, as Tertullian said, simplicity and power are the constant marks of God's work—simplicity in method, power in effect.

CHAPTER VII

JESUS' TEACHING UPON SIN

"For clear-thinking ethical natures," writes a modern scholar, "for natures such as those of Jesus and St. Paul, it is a downright necessity to separate heaven and hell as distinctly as possible. It is only ethically worthless speculations that have always tried to minimize this distinction. Carlyle is an instance in our times of how men even to-day once more enthusiastically welcome the conception of hell as soon as the distinction between good and bad becomes all-important to them."[1]

Here in strong terms a challenge is put to many of our current ideas. Is not this to revert to an outworn view of the Christian religion—to reassert its dark side, better forgotten, all the horrible emphasis on sin and its consequences introduced into the sunny teaching of Jesus by Paul of Tarsus, and alien to it? Before we answer this question in any direct way, it is worth while to realize for how many of the real thinkers, and the great teachers of mankind, this distinction between good and evil has been fundamental. They have not invented it as a theory on which to base religion, but they have found it in human life, one and all of them. If Walt Whitman or Swami Vivekananda overlook the difference between virtue and vice, and do honor to the

[1] Wernle, *Beginnings of Christianity* (vol. i. p. 286, English translation).

courtesan, it simply means that they are bad thinkers, bad observers. The deeper minds see more clearly and escape the confusion into which the slight and quick, the sentimental, hurl themselves. Above all, when God in any degree grows real to a man, when a man seriously gives himself not to some mere vague "contemplation" of God but to the earnest study of God's ways in human affairs, and of God's laws and their working, the great contrasts in men's responses to God's rule become luminous.

When God matters to a man, all life shows the result. Good and bad, right and wrong stand out clear as the contrast between light and darkness—they cannot be mistaken, and they matter—and matter for ever. They are no concern of a moment. Action makes character; and, until the action is undone again, the effect on character is not undone. Right and wrong are of eternal significance now in virtue of the reality of God.

Gautama Buddha, for instance, and the greater Hindu thinkers, in their doctrine of *Karma*, have taught a significance inherent in good and evil, which we can only not call boundless. Buddha did this without any great consciousness of God; and many Indian thinkers have so emphasized the doctrine that it has taken all the stress laid on *Bhakti* by Ramanuja and others to restore to life a perspective or a balance, however it should be described, that will save men from utter despair. Nor is it Eastern thinkers only who have taught men the reality of heaven and hell. The poetry of Æschylus is full of his great realization of the nexus between act and outcome. With all the humor and charm there is in Plato, we cannot escape his tremendous teaching on the age-long consequences of good and evil in a cosmos ordered by God. Carlyle, in our own days, realized the same thing—he learnt it no doubt from his mother; and learnt it again in London. In Mrs. Austen's drawing-room, with "Sidney Smith guffawing," and "other people prating, jargoning, to me through these thin cobwebs Death and Eternity sate glaring." "How will this look in the Universe," he asks, "and before the Creator of Man?" When someone in his old age challenged him with the question, "Who will be judge?"—(it is curious how every sapient inanity strikes, as on an original idea, on the notion that opinions differ, and therefore —apparently, if their thought *has* any consequence— are as good one as another)—Who will be judge? "Hell fire will be judge," said Carlyle, "God Almighty will be the judge now and always." There is a gulf between good and evil, and each is inexorably fertile of consequence. There is no escaping the issue of moral choice. That is the conclusion of men who have handled human experience in a serious spirit. As physical laws are deducible from the reactions of matter and force, and are found to be uniform and inevitable, fundamental in the nature of matter and force, so clear-thinking men in the course of ages have deduced moral laws from their observation of human nature, laws as uniform, inevitable and fundamental. In neither case has it been that men invented or imagined the laws; in both cases it has been genuine discovery of what was already existent and operative, and often the discovery has involved surprise.

If Jesus had failed to see laws so fundamental, which other teachers of mankind have recognized, it is hardly likely that his teaching would have survived or influenced men as it has done. Mankind can dispense with a teacher who misses patent facts, whatever his charm. But there never was any doubt that Jesus was alive to the difference between right and wrong. His critics saw this, but they held that he confused moral issues, and that his distinctions in the ethical sphere were badly drawn.

Jesus could not have ignored the problem of sin and forgiveness, even if he had wished to ignore it. To this the thought of mankind had been gravitating, and in Jewish and in Greek thought conduct was more and more the center of everything. For the Stoics morals were the dominant part of philosophy; but for our present purpose we need not go outside the literature of the New Testament. Sin was the keynote of the preaching of John the Baptist. It is customary to connect the mission of Jesus with that of John, and to find in the Baptist's preaching either the announcement of his Successor (as is said with most emphasis in the Fourth Gospel), or (as some now say) the impulse which drove Jesus of Nazareth into his public ministry. Whatever may be the historical connection between them, it is as important for us at least to realize the broad gulf that separates them. They meet, it is true; both use the phrase "Kingdom of God," both preach repentance in view of the coming of the Kingdom; and we are apt to assume they mean the same thing; but Jesus took some pains to make it clear, though in the gentlest and most sympathetic way, that they did not.

On the famous occasion, when John the Baptist sent two of his disciples to Jesus with his striking message: "Art thou he that should come? or look we for another?"

(Luke vii. 19-35; Matt. xi. 1-19), Jesus, when the messengers were gone, spoke to the people about the Baptist. "What went ye out into the wilderness for to see? A reed shaken with the wind? A man clothed in soft raiment? A prophet? Yea, I say unto you, and much more than a prophet. Among those that are born of women there is not a greater prophet than John the Baptist, but he that is least in the Kingdom of God is greater than he." I am not sure which is the right translation, whether it is "he that is less, least, or little," and I do not propose to discuss it. The judgment is remarkable enough in any case, and the words of Jesus, as we have seen, have a close relation to real fact as he saw it. Why does he speak in this way? Our answer to this question, if we can answer it, will help us forward to the larger problem before us. But, for this, we shall have to study John with some care.

There is a growing agreement among scholars that there is some confusion in our data as to John the Baptist. There are gaps in the record—for instance, how and why did the school of John survive as it did (Acts xviii. 25, xix. 1-7)? And again there are, in the judgment of some, developments of the story. The Gospel, with varying degrees of explicitness, and St. Paul by inference (Acts xix. 4) tell us that John pointed to "him which should come after him." Christians, at any rate, after the Resurrection, had no doubt that this was Jesus. Whether John was as definite as the narratives now represent him to have been, has been doubted in view of his message to Jesus. But that is not our present subject. We are concerned less with John as precursor than as teacher and thinker.

Even if our data are defective, still enough is given us to let us see a very striking and commanding figure. We have a picture of him, his dress, his diet, his style of speech, his method of action—in every way he is a signal and arresting man. The son of a priest, he is an ascetic, who lives in the wilderness, dresses like a peasant, and eats the meanest and most meager of food—a man of the desert and of solitude. And the whole life reacts on him and we can see him, lean and worn, though still a young man, a keen, rather excitable spirit—in every feature the marks of revolt against a civilization which he views as an apostasy. Luke, using a phrase from the Old Testament, says, "The word of God came upon John in the wilderness" (Luke iii. 2). Luke leans to Old Testament phrase, and here is one that hits off the man to the very life. Jesus himself confirms Luke's judgment (Mark xi. 29-33). The Word of the Lord has come on this ascetic figure, and he goes to the people with the message; he draws their attention and they crowd out to see him. He makes a great sensation. He is not like other men—for Jesus quotes their remark that "he had a devil" (Luke vii. 33) —a rough and ready way of explaining unlikeness to the average man. When he sees his congregation his words are not conciliatory; he addresses them as a "generation of vipers" (Luke iii. 7); and his text is the "wrath to come."

Jesus asks whether they went out to see a reed shaken by the wind, or someone dressed like a courtier—the last things to which anyone would compare John. There was nothing supple about him, as Herod found, and Herodias (Mark vi. 17-20); he was not shaken by the wind; there was no trimming of his sails. The austerity of his life and the austerity of his spirit go together, and he preached in a tone and a language that scorched. He preached righteousness, social righteousness, and he did it in a great way. He brought back the minds of his people, like Amos and others, to God's conceptions and away from their own. Crowds of people went out to hear him (Mark i. 5),[1] and he made a deep impression on many whose lives needed amendment (Matt. xxi. 26, 32; Luke xx. 6). We have the substance of what he said in the third chapter of St. Luke; how he told the tax-collectors to be honest and not make things worse than they need be; the soldiers to do violence to no man and accuse no man falsely, and to be content with their wages; and to ordinary people he preached humanity: "He that hath two coats, let him impart to him that hath none; and he that hath meat, let him do likewise." It may be remarked of John, and it is true also of Jesus, that neither attacked the absent nor inveighed against economic conditions, as some modern preachers do with, let us say, capitalists and the morality of other nations. Neither says a word against the Roman Empire. Slavery is not condemned explicitly even by Jesus, though he gave the dynamic that abolished it. The practical guidance that John gave, he gave in response to men's inquiries.

Like an Old Testament prophet (*cf.* Amos iii. 2), John tore to tatters any plea that could be offered that his listeners were God's chosen people, the children of Abraham. Does God want children of Abraham?—John pointed to the stones on the ground, and said, if God

[1] So too says Josephus, who gives this as the reason of Herod's suspicion of him.

wanted, he could make children of Abraham out of them; a word and he could have as many children of Abraham as he wished. It was something else that God sought.

"John," writes the historian Josephus a generation later, "was a good man, and commanded the Jews to exercise virtue both in justice toward one another and piety towards God, and so to come to baptism; for so baptism would be acceptable to God if they made use of it, not to excuse certain sins, but for the purification of the body, provided that the soul was thoroughly purified beforehand by righteousness."[1] This interpretation of John's baptism makes it look very like the baptisms and other purificatory rites of the heathen. The Gospels attribute to John a message, richer and more powerful, but essentially the same; and the criticism of Jesus confirms the account. The great note in his preaching is judgment; the Kingdom of God is coming, and it begins with judgment. Again, it is like Amos—"The axe is at the root of the tree," "His fan is in His hand." And as men listened to the man and looked at him—his intense belief in his message, backed up by a stern self-discipline, a whole life inspired, infused by conviction—they believed this message of the axe, the fan, and the fire. They asked and as we have seen received his guidance on the conduct of life; they accepted his baptism, and set about the amending of character (Matt. xxi. 32).

Jesus makes it quite clear that he held John to be an entirely exceptional man, and that he had no doubt that

---

[1] *Antiquities of the Jews*, xviii. 5, 2, § 117, *cf.* what Celsus says of righteousness as a condition of admission to certain mysteries that offer forgiveness of sins (Origen, *c. Celsum*, iii. 59). The "purification of the body" has a ritual and ceremonial significance.

John's teaching was from God (Matt. xxi. 32; Luke vii. 35, xx. 4; and, of course, Luke vii. 26-28). It was all in the line of the great prophets; and the Fourth Gospel shows it us once more in the work of the Holy Spirit—"when he is come, he will reprove (convict) the world of sin, and of righteousness, and of judgment" (John xvi. 8). And yet, as Jesus says, there is all the difference in the world between his own Gospel and the teaching of the Baptist.

In Mark's narrative (ii. 18) a very significant episode is recorded. John inculcated fasting, and his disciples fasted a great deal (*pykna*, Luke v. 33); and once, Mark tells us, when they were actually fasting, they asked Jesus why his disciples did not do the same? Jesus' answer is a little cryptic at first sight. "Can the children of the bridechamber fast, while the bridegroom is with them?" Who fasts at the wedding feast, in the hour of gladness? And then he passes on to speak about the new patch on the old garment, the new wine in the old wine skins; and it looks as if it were not merely a criticism of John's disciples but of John himself. John, indeed, brings home with terrific force and conviction that truth of God which the prophets had preached before; but he leaves it there. He emphasizes once more the old laws of God, the judgments of God, but he brings no transforming power into men's lives. The old characters, the old motives more or less, are to be patched by a new fear.

"Repent, repent," John cries, "the judgment is coming." And men do repent, and John baptizes them as a symbol that God has forgiven them. But how are they to go on? What is the power that is to carry John's disciples through the rest of their lives? We are not in possession of everything that John says, but there is no indication that John had very much to say about any force or power that should keep men on the plane of repentance. It is our experience that we repent and fall again; what else was the experience of the people whom John baptized? What was to keep them on the new level—not only in the isolation of the desert, but in the ordinary routine of town and village? In John's teaching there is not a word about that; and this is a weakness of double import. For, as Jesus puts it, the new patch on the old garment makes the rent worse; it does not leave it merely as it was. If the "unclean spirit" regain its footing in a man, it does not come alone—"the last state of that man is worse than the first" (Luke xi. 24-26). Jesus is very familiar with the type that welcomes new ideas and new impulses in religion and yet does nothing, grows tired or afraid, and relapses (Mark iv. 17).

Again, in John's teaching, as far as we have it, there is a striking absence of any clear word about any relation to God, beyond that of debtor and creditor, judge and prisoner on trial, king and subject. God may forgive and God will judge; but so far as our knowledge of John's teaching goes, these are the only two points at which man and God will touch each other; and these are not intimate relations. There is no promise and no gladness in them; no "good news." John taught prayer—all sorts of people teach prayer; but what sort of prayer? It has been remarked of the Greek poet, Apollonius Rhodius, that his heroes used prayers, but their prayers were like official documents. Of what character were the prayers that John taught his disciples? None of them survive; but there is perhaps a tacit criticism of them in the request made to the New Teacher: "Teach us to pray, as John taught his disciples" (Luke xi. 1). One feels that the men wanted something different from John's prayers. Great and strenuous prayers they may have been, but in marked contrast to the prayers of Jesus and his followers, because of the absence in John's message of any strong note of the love and tenderness of God.

Finally, the very righteousness that John preaches with such fire and energy is open to criticism. Far more serious than the righteousness of the Pharisees, stronger in insight and more generous in its scope, it fails in the same way; it is self-directed. It aims at a man's own salvation, and it is to be achieved by a man's own strength in self-discipline, with what little help John's system of prayer and fasting may win for a man from God. John fails precisely where his strength is greatest and most conspicuous. His theme is sin; his emphasis all falls on sin; but his psychology of sin is insufficient, it is not deep enough. The simple, strenuous ascetic did not realize the seriousness of sin after all—its deep roots, its haunting power, its insidious charm. St. Paul saw far deeper into it—"I am carnal, sold under sin. What I hate that do I. The good that I would, I do not; but the evil which I would not, that I do. I see a law in my members bringing me into captivity to the law of sin. O wretched man that I am! Who shall deliver me from the body of this death?" (Rom. vii. 14-24). Sin, in John's thought, is contumacy or rebellion against the law of God; he does not look at it in relation to the love of God—a view of it which gives it another character altogether. Nor has John any great conception of forgiveness—a man, he thinks, may win it by "fruits worthy of repentance" (Luke iii. 8). Here again Paul is the pioneer in the universal Christian experience that fruits of repentance can never buy God's forgiveness. That is God's gift. That forgiveness may cost a man much—an amended life, the practices of prayer and fasting and almsgiving—John conceives; but we are not led to think that he thought of what it might cost God. John has no evangel, no really good news, with gladness and singing in it (I Peter i. 8).

When we return to the teaching of Jesus, we find that he draws a clear and sharp line between right and wrong. He indicates that right is right to the end of all creation, and wrong is wrong up to the very Judgment Throne of God (Matt. xxv.). He views these things, as the old phrase puts it, *sub specie æternitatis*, from the outlook of eternity. Right and wrong do not meet at infinity. There is no higher synthesis that can make them one and the same thing. Everything with Jesus is Theocentric, and until God changes there will be no very great change in right and wrong. Partly because he uses the language of his day, partly because he thinks as a rule in pictures, his language is apt to be misconstrued by moderns. But the central ideas are clear enough. "How are you to escape the judgment of Gehenna?" he asks the Pharisees (Matt. xxiii. 33; the subjunctive mood is worth study). It is not a threat, but a question. There yawns the chasm; with your driving, how *do* you think you can avoid disaster? He warns men of a doom where the worm dies not and the fire is not quenched; a man will do well to sacrifice hand, foot or eye, to save the rest of himself from that (Mark ix. 43-48). But a more striking picture, though commonly less noticed, he draws or suggests in talk at the last supper. "Simon, Simon, behold Satan asked for you to sift you as wheat, but I prayed for thee, that thy faith fail not; and thou, when thou comest back, strengthen thy brethren" (Luke xxii. 31, 32). The scene suggested is not unlike that at the beginning of the Book of Job, or that in the Book of Zechariah (chap. iii.). There is the throne of God, and into that Presence pushes Satan with a demand—the verb in the Greek is a strong one, though not so strong as the Revised Version suggests. Satan "made a push to have you." "But I prayed for thee." To any reader who has any feeling or imagination, what do these short sentences mean? What can they mean, from the lips of a thinker so clear and so serious, and a friend so tender? What but unspeakable peril? The language has for us a certain strangeness; but it shows plainly enough that, to Jesus' mind, the disciples, and Peter in particular, stood in danger, a danger so urgent that it called for the Saviour's prayer. So much it meant to him, and he himself tells Peter what he had realized, what he had done, in language that could not be mistaken or forgotten. To the nature of the danger that sin involves, we shall return. Meanwhile we may consider what Jesus means by sin before we discuss its consequences.

"The Son of Man," says Jesus, in a sentence that is famous but still insufficiently studied, "is come to seek and to save that which is lost" (Luke xix. 10). Our rule has been to endeavor to give to the terms of Jesus the connotation he meant them to carry. The scholar will linger over the "Son of Man"—a difficult phrase, with a literary and linguistic history that is very complicated. For the present purpose the significant words are at the other end of the sentence. What does Jesus mean by "lost"? It is a strong word, the value of which we have in some degree lost through familiarity. And whom would he describe as "lost"? We have once more to recall his criticism of Peter—that Peter "thought like a man and not like God" (Mark viii. 33)—and to be on our guard lest we think too quickly and too slightly. We may remark, too, that for Jesus sin is not, as for Paul and theologians in general, primarily an intellectual problem. He does not use the abstraction Sin as Paul does. But the clear, steady gaze turned on men and women misses little.

There are four outstanding classes, whom he warns of the danger of hell in one form or other.

To begin, there is the famous description of the Last Judgment (Matt. xxv. 31-46)—a description in itself not altogether new. Plenty of writers and thinkers had described the scene, and the broad outlines of the picture were naturally common property; yet it is to these more or less conventional traits that attention has often been too exclusively devoted. Jesus, however, altered the whole character of the Judgment Day scene by his account of the principles on which the Judge decides the cases brought before him. On the right hand of the Judge are—not the Jews confronting the Gentiles on the left—nor exactly the well-conducted and well-balanced people who get there in Greek allegories—but a group of men and women who realize where they are with a gasp of surprise. How has it come about? The Judge tells them: "I was an hungered and ye gave me meat," and the rest of the familiar words. But this does not quite settle the question. Embarrassment rises on their faces—is it a mistake? One of them speaks for the rest: "Lord, when saw we thee an hungered and fed thee?" They do not remember it. There is something characteristic there of the whole school of Jesus; these people are "children of fact," honest as their Master, and they will not accept heaven in virtue of a possible mistake. And it appears from the Judge's answer that such instinctive deeds go further than men think, even if they are forgotten. Wordsworth speaks of the "little nameless unremembered acts of kindness and of love" that are "the best portion of a good man's life."[1] The acts of kindness were forgotten just because they were instinctive, but, Jesus emphasizes the point, they are decisive; they come, as another of his telling phrases suggests, from "the overflow of the heart," and they reveal it. With the people on the left hand it was the other way. They were fairly well in possession of their good records, but they had missed the decisive fact—they were instinctively hard. Such people Jesus warns. So familiar are his words that there is a danger of our limiting them to their first obvious meaning. Eighty years ago Thomas Carlyle looked out on the England he knew, and remarked that it was strange that the great battle of civilized man should be still the battle of the savage against famine, and with that he observed that the people were "needier than ever of inward sustenance." Is there a warning in this picture of the people on the left hand that applies to deeper things than physical hunger? A warning to those who do not heed another's need of "inward sustenance," of spiritual life, of God? It looks likely. Otherwise there is a risk of our declining upon a "Social Righteousness" that falls a long way short of John the Baptist's, and does less for any soul, our own or another's.

---

[1] *Lines Composed above Tintern*, 34.

The second class warned by Jesus consists of several groups dealt with in the Sermon on the Mount—people whose sin is not murder or adultery, but merely anger and the unclean thought—not the people who actually give themselves away, like the publicans and harlots—but those who would not be sorry to have that ring of Gyges which Plato described, who would like to do certain things if they could, who at all events are not unwilling to picture what they would wish to do, if it were available, and meanwhile enjoy the thought (Matt. v. 21, 22, 27-29). Here St. Paul can supply commentary with his suggestion that one form of God's condemnation is where he gives up a man to his own reprobate mind (Romans i. 28—the whole passage is worth study in the Greek). The mind, in Paul's phrases, becomes darkened (Rom. i. 21), stained (Titus i. 15), and cauterized (1 Tim. iv. 2), invalidated for the discharge of its proper functions, as a burnt hand loses the sense of touch, or a stained glass gives the man a blue or red world instead of the real one. Blindness and mutilation are better, Jesus said, than the eye of lust (Matt. v. 28). How different from the moralists, for whom sin lies in action, and all actions are physical! The idle word is to condemn a man, not because it is idle, but because, being unstudied, it speaks of his heart and reveals, unconsciously but plainly, what he *is* in reality (Matt. xii. 36). Thus it is that what comes out of the mouth defiles a man (Matt. xv. 18)—with the curious suggestion, whether intended or not, that the formulation of a floating thought gives it new power to injure or to help.[1] That is true; impression loose, as it were, in the mind,

---

[1] See end of Chapter II.

mere thought-stuff, is one thing; formulated, brought to phrase and form, it takes on new life and force; and when it is evil, it does defile, and in a permanent way. Marcus Aurelius has a very similar warning (v. 16)—"Whatever the color of the thoughts often before thy mind, that color will thy mind take. For the mind is dyed (or stained) by its thoughts." *Phantazesthai* and *phantasiai* are the words —and they suggest something between thoughts and imaginations—mental pictures would be very near it.

The third group whom Jesus warned, the most notorious of all, was the Pharisee class. They played at religion—tithed mint and anise and cummin, and forgot judgment and mercy and faith (Matt. xxiii. 23). Jesus said that the Pharisee was never quite sure whether the creature he was looking at was a camel or a mosquito—he got them mixed (Matt. xxiii. 24). Once we realize what this tremendous irony means, we are better able to grasp his thought. The Pharisee was living in a world that was *not* the real one—it was a highly artificial one, picturesque and charming no doubt, but dangerous. For, after all, we do live in the real world—there is only one world, however many we may invent; and to live in any other is danger. Blindness, that is partial and uneven, lands a man in peril whenever he tries to come downstairs or to cross the street—he steps on the doorstep that is not there and misses the real one. He is involved in false appearances at every turn. And so it is in the moral world—there is one real, however many unreals there are, and to trust to the unreal is to come to grief on the real. "The beginning of a man's doom," wrote Carlyle, "is that vision be withdrawn from him." "Thou blind Pharisee!" (Matt. xxiii. 26). The cup is clean enough without; it is septic and poisonous within—and from which side of it do you drink, outside or inside? (Matt. xxiii. 25). As we study the teaching of Jesus here, we see anew the profundity of the saying attributed to him in the Fourth Gospel, "The truth shall make you free" (John viii. 32). The man with astigmatism, or myopia, or whatever else it is, must get the glasses that will show him the real world, and he is safe, and free to go and come as he pleases. See the real in the moral sphere, and the first great peril is gone. Nothing need be said at this point of the Pharisee who used righteousness and long prayers as a screen for villainy. Probably his doom was that in the end he came to think his righteousness and his prayers real, and to reckon them as credit with a God, who did not see through them any more than he did himself. It is a mistake to over-emphasize here the devouring of widow' houses by the Pharisee (Matt. xxiii. 14), for it was no peculiar weakness of his; publicans and unjust judges did the same. Only the publican and the unjust judge told themselves no lies about it. The Pharisee lied—lying to oneself or lying to another, which is the worse? The more dangerous probably is lying to oneself, though the two practices generally will go together in the long run. The worst forms of lying, then, are lying to oneself and lying about God; and the Pharisee combined them, and told himself that, once God's proper dues of prayer and tithe were paid, his treatment of the widow and her house was correct. Hence, says Jesus, he receives "greater damnation" (A.V.)—or judgment on a higher scale (*perissoteron krima*).

The Pharisees were men who believed in God—only that with his world, they re-created him (as we are all apt to do for want of vision or by choice); but what is atheism, what can it be, but indifference to God's facts and to God's nature? If religion is union with God, in the phrase we borrow so slightly from the mystics, how can a man be in union with God, when the god he sees is not there, is a figment of his own mind, something different altogether from God? Or, if we use the phrase of the Old Testament prophet and of Jesus himself, if religion is vision of God, what is our religion, if after all we are not seeing God at all, but something else—a dummy god, like that of the Pharisees, some trifling martinet who can be humbugged—or, to come to ourselves, a majestic bundle of abstract nouns loosely tied up in impersonality? For all such Jesus has a caution. Indifference to God's facts leads to one end only. We admit it ourselves. There are those who scold Bunyan for sending Ignorance to hell, but we omit to ask where else could Ignorance go, whether Bunyan sent him or not. Ignorance, as to germs or precipices or what not, leads to destruction *in pari materia*; in the moral sphere can it be otherwise? This serves in some measure to explain why Jesus is so tender to gross and flagrant sinners, a fact which some have noted with surprise. Surely it is because publican and harlot have fewer illusions; they were left little chance of imagining their lives to be right before God. What Jesus thought of their hardness and impurity we have seen already, but heedless as they were of God's requirements of them, they were not guilty of the intricate atheism of the Pharisees. Further, whether it was in his mind or not, it is also true that the frankly gross temptations do bring a man face to face with his own need of God, as the subtler do not; and so far they make for reality.

The fourth group are those who cannot make up their minds. "No man, having put his hand to the plough, and looking back, is fit for the Kingdom of God" (Luke ix. 62). The word is an interesting one (*euthetos*), it means "handy" or "easy to place."[1] This man is not adapted for the Kingdom of God; he is not easy to place there. Like the man who saved his talent but did not use it (Matt. xxv. 24), he is not exactly bad; but he is "no good," as we say. Jesus conceives of the Kingdom of God as dynamic, not static; state or place, condition or relation, it implies work, as God himself implies work. He holds that truth is not a curiosity for the cabinet but a tool in the hand; that God's earnest world is no place for nondescript, and that there is only one region left to which they can drift. What part or place can there be in the Kingdom of Heaven—in a kingdom won on Calvary—for people who cannot be relied on, who cannot decide whether to plough or not to plough, nor, when they have made up their mind, stick to it? Jesus cannot see. What a revelation of the force and power of his own character!

These, then, are the four classes whom Jesus warns, and it is clear from the consideration of them that his view of sin is very different from those current in that day. Men set sin down as an external thing that drifted on to one like a floating burr—or like paint, perhaps—it could be picked off or burnt off. It was the eating of pork or hare—something technical or accidental; or it was, many thought, the work of a demon from without,

---

[1] The word is used of the salt not "fit" for land or dunghill (Luke xiv. 35), and the negative of the inconvenient harbor (Acts xxvii. 12).

who could be driven out to whence he came. Love and drunkenness illustrated the thing for them—a change of personality induced by an exterior force or object, as if the human spirit were a glass or a cup into which anything might be poured, and from which it could be emptied and the vessel itself remain unaffected. Jesus has a deeper view of sin, a stronger psychology, than these, nor does he, like some quick thinkers of to-day, put sin down to a man's environment, as if certain surroundings inevitably meant sin. Jesus is quite definite that sin is nothing accidental—it is involved in a man's own nature, in his choice, it comes from the heart, and it speaks of a heart that is wrong.

When we survey the four groups, it comes to one central question at last: Has a man been in earnest with himself about God's dealings with him? Hardness and lust make a man play the fool with human souls whom God loves and cares for—a declaration of war on God himself. Wilful self-deception about God needs no comment; to shilly-shally and let decision slide, where God is concerned, is atheism too. In a word, what is a man's fundamental attitude to God and God's facts? That is Jesus' question. Sin is tracked home to the innermost and most essential part of the man—his will. It is no outward thing, it is inward. It is not that evil befalls us, but that we *are* evil. In the words of Edward Caird, "the passion that misleads us is a manifestation of the same *ego*, the same self-conscious reason which is misled by it," and thus, as Burns puts it, "it is the very 'light from heaven' that leads us astray." The man uses his highest God-given faculties, and uses them against God.

But this is not all. Many people will agree with the estimate of Jesus, when they understand it, in regard to most of these classes; perhaps they would urge that in the main it is substantially the same teaching as John the Baptist's, though it implies, as we shall see, a more difficult problem in getting rid of sin. Jesus goes further. He holds up to men standards of conduct which transcend anything yet put before mankind. "Be ye therefore perfect," he says, "even as your Father which is in heaven is perfect" (Matt. v. 48). When we recall what Jesus teaches of God, when we begin to try to give to "God" the content he intended, we realize with amazement what he is saying. He is holding up to men for their ideal of conduct the standard of God's holiness, of God's love and tenderness. Everything that Jesus tells us of God—all that he has to say of the wonderful and incredible love of God and of God's activity on behalf of his children—he now incorporates in the ideal of conduct to which men are called. John's conceptions of righteousness grow beggarly. Here is a royal magnificence of active love, of energetic sympathy, tenderness, and self-giving, asked of us, who find it hard enough to keep the simplest commandments from our youth up (Mark x. 20). We are to love our enemies, to win them, to make peace, to be pure—and all on the scale of God. And that this may not seem mere talk in the air, there is the character and personality of Jesus, embodying all he asks of us—bringing out new wonders of God's goodness, the ugliness and evil of sin, and the positive and redemptive beauty of righteousness.

The problem of sin and forgiveness becomes more difficult, as we think of the positive ideals which we have not begun to try to reach. Let us sum up what it involves.

Jesus brings out the utter bankruptcy to which sin reduces men. They become "full of hypocrisy and lawlessness" (Matt. xxiii. 28), so depraved that they are like bad trees, unproductive of any but bad fruit (rotten, in the Greek, Matt. vii. 17); the very light in them is darkness, and how great darkness (Matt. vi. 23). They are cut off from the real world, as we saw, and lose the faculties they have abused—the talent is taken away (Matt. xxv. 28); "from him that hath not, shall be taken away even that which he hath" (Matt. xxv. 29). The nature is changed as memory is changed, and the "overflow of the heart" in speech and act bears witness to it. The faculty of choice is weakened; the interval in which inhibition—to use our modern term—is possible, grows shorter. The instincts are perverted and the whole being is disorganized. In a word, all that Jesus connotes by "the Kingdom of God" is "taken from them" (Matt. xxi. 43), and nothing left but "outer darkness" (Matt. xxii. 13). The vision of God is not for the impure (Matt. v. 8). Meanwhile sin is not a sterile thing, it is a leaven (Matt. xvi. 6). If our modern medical language may be applied—and Jesus used the analogy of medicine in this very case (Mark ii. 17)—sin is septic. In the first place, all sin is anti-social—an invasion *ipso facto* of the rights of others. The man who sins either takes away what is another's—a man's goods, a widow's house, or a woman's purity—or he fails to give to others what is their due, be it, in the obvious field, the aid the Good Samaritan rendered to the wounded and robbed man by the roadside (Luke x. 33), or, in the higher sphere, truth, sympathy, help in the maintenance of principle, or in the achievement of progress and development (*cf.* Matt. xxv. 43). Sin is the repudiation of the concepts of law, duty, and service, in a word, of the love on God's scale which God calls men to exercise. And its fruits are, above all, its dissemination. Injustice, a historian has said, always repays itself with frightful compound interest. If a man starts to debauch society, his example is quickly followed; and it comes to hatred.

What, we asked, did Jesus mean by "lost"? This, above all, that sin cuts a man adrift from God. In the parable of the Prodigal Son this is brought out (Luke xv. 11-32). There the youth took from his father all he could get, and then deliberately turned his back on him forever; he went into a far country, out of his reach, outside his influence, and beyond the range of his ideas, and he devoted his father's gifts to precisely what would sadden and trouble his father most. And then came bankruptcy, final and hopeless. There was no father available in the far country; he had to live without him, and it came to a life that was not even human—a life of solitude, a life of beasts. Jesus draws it, as he does most things, in picture form, using parable. Paul puts the same in directer language—sin reduces men to a position where they are "alienated from the life of God" (Eph. iv. 18; Col. i. 21), "without God in the world" (Eph. ii. 12), "enemies of God" (Rom. v. 10; Col. i. 21); but he does not say more than Jesus implies. Paul's final expression, "God gave them up" (thrice in Rom. i. 24, 26, 28), answers to the Judge's word, in Jesus' picture, "Depart from me" (Matt. xxv. 41).

O Wedding-guest, this soul hath been
  Alone on a wide, wide sea:
So lonely 'twas, that God himself
  Scarce seemèd there to be.

So Jesus handles the problem of sin, but that is only half the story, for there remains the problem of Redemption. The treatment of sin is far profounder and truer than John the Baptist or any other teacher has achieved; and it implies that Jesus will handle Redemption in a way no less profound and effective. If he does not, then he had better not have preached a gospel. If in dealing with sin he touches reality at every point, we may expect him in the matter of Redemption to reach the very center of life.[1] How else can he, with his serious view of sin, say to a man, "Thy sins are forgiven thee"? (Mark ii. 5). But it is quite clear from our records that, while Jesus laid bare in this relentless way the ugliness and hopelessness of sin, he did not despair: his tone is always one of hope and confidence. The strong man armed may find a stronger man come upon him and take from him the panoply in which he trusted (Luke xi. 21, 22). There is a great gulf that cannot be crossed (Luke xvi. 26)—yes, but if the experience of Christendom tells us anything, it tells us that Jesus crossed it himself, and did the impossible. "The great matter is that Jesus believed God was willing to take the human soul, and make it new and young and clean again." But the human soul did not believe it, till Jesus convinced it, and won it, by action of his own. "The Son of Man came to seek and to save that which was lost"; and he did not come in vain.

[1] That he did so is emphasized again and again, in striking language, by St. Paul—*e.g.* Rom. v. 15-16, 20; 1 Tim. i. 14.

CHAPTER VIII

THE CHOICE OF THE CROSS

By what they said, I perceived that he had been a great warrior, and had fought with and slain him that had the power of death (Heb. ii. 14), but not without great danger to himself, which made me love him the more.—*Pilgrim's Progress*, Part I.

THE subject before us is one of the greatest difficulty. Why Jesus chose the cross has exercised the thought of the Christian world ever since he did so. He told his disciples beforehand of what lay before him, of what he was choosing, but it was long before they realized that he meant any such thing. The cross was to them a strange idea, and for a long time they did not seriously face the matter. Once the cross was an accomplished fact, Christians could not, and did not wish to, avoid thinking out what had meant so much to their Master; but it has mostly been with a sense of facing a mystery that in some measure eluded them, with a feeling that there is more beyond, something always to be attained hereafter.

A very significant passage in St. Mark (x. 32) gives us a glimpse of a moment on Jesus' last journey to Jerusalem. It is a sentence which one could hardly imagine being included in the Gospel, if it did not represent some actual memory, and a memory of significance. It runs something like this: "And they were in the way, going up to Jerusalem, and Jesus was moving on before them; and they began to wonder; and as they followed they began to be afraid." He is moving to Jerusalem with a purpose. They do not understand it. He is wrapped in thought; and, as happens when a man's mind is working strongly, his pace quickens, and they find themselves at a distance behind him. And then something comes over them—a sense that there is something in the situation which they do not understand, a strangeness in the mind. They realize, in fact, that they are not as near Jesus as they had supposed. And, as they follow, the wonder deepens into fear.

Anyone who will really try to grapple with this problem of the cross will find very soon the same thing. The first thing that we need to learn, if our criticism of Jesus is to be sound, is that we are not at all so near him as we have imagined. He eludes us, goes far out beyond what we grasp or conceive; and I think the education of the Christian man or woman begins anew, when we realize how little we know about Jesus. The discovery of our ignorance is the beginning of knowledge. Plato long ago said that wonder is the mother of philosophy, and he was right. John Donne, the English poet, went farther, and said: "All divinity is love or wonder." When a man then begins to wonder about Jesus Christ in earnest, Jesus comes to be for him a new figure. Historical criticism has done this for us; it has brought us to such a point that the story of these earliest disciples repeats itself more closely in the experience of their followers of these days than in any century since the first. We begin along with them on the friendly, critical, human plane, and with them we follow him into experiences and realizations that we never expected. It may be summed up in the familiar words of the English hymn,

> Oh happy band of pilgrims,
> If onward ye will tread
> With Jesus as your fellow,
> To Jesus as your head.

These men begin with him, more or less on a footing of equality; or, at least, the inequality is very lightly marked. Afterwards it is emphasized; and they realize it with wonder and with fear, and at last with joy and gratitude.

We may begin by trying steadily to bring our minds to some keener sense of what it was that he chose. To say, in the familiar words, that he chose the cross, may through the very familiarity of the language lead us away from what we have to discover. We have, as we agreed, to ask ourselves what was his experience. What, then, did his choice involve? It meant, of course, physical pain. There are natures to whom this is of little account, but the sensitive and sentient type, as we often observe, dreads pain. He, with open eyes, chose physical pain, heightened to torture, not escaping any of the suffering which anticipation gives—that physical horror of death, that instinctive fear of annihilation, which nature suggests of itself. He took the course of action that would most severely test his disciples; one at least revolted, and we have to ask what it meant to Jesus to live with Judas, to watch his face, to recognize his influence in the little group—yes, and to try to win him again and to be repelled. "He learnt by the things that he suffered" that Judas would betray him; but the hour and place and method were not so evident, and when they were at last revealed—what did it mean to be kissed by Judas? Do we feel what he felt in the so-called trials—or was he dull and numbed by the catastrophe? How did he bear the beating of triumphant hatred upon a forsaken spirit? How did the horrible cry, "Crucify him! crucify him!" break on his ears—on his mind? When "the Lord turned and looked upon Peter" (Luke xxii. 61), what did it mean? How did he know that Peter was there, and what led him to turn at that moment? Was there in the Passion no element of uneasiness again about the eleven on whom he had concentrated his hopes and his influence—the eleven of whom it is recorded, that "they all forsook him, and fled" (Mark xiv. 50)? No hint of dread that his work might indeed be undone? What pain must that have involved? What is the value of the Agony in the Garden, of the cry, "*Eloi, Eloi, lama sabachthani*" (Mark xv. 34)? When we have answered, each for himself, these questions, and others like them that will suggest themselves—answered them by the most earnest efforts of which our natures are capable—and remembered at the end how far our natures fall short of his, and told ourselves that our answers are insufficient—then let us recall, once more, that he chose all this.

He chose the cross and all that it meant. Our next step should be to study anew his own references to what he intends by it, to what he expects to be its results and its outcome. First of all, then, he clearly means that the Kingdom of Heaven is something different from anything that man has yet seen. The Kingdom of Heaven is, I understand, a Hebrew way of saying the Kingdom of God—very much as men to-day speak of Providence, to avoid undue familiarity with the term God, so the Jews would say Heaven. There were many who used the phrase in one or other form; but it is always bad criticism to give to the words of genius the value or the connotation they would have in the lips of ordinary people. To a great mind words are charged with a fulness of meaning that little people do not reach. The attempt has been made to recapture more of his thoughts by learning the value given to some of the terms he uses as they appear in the literature of the day, and of course it has been helpful. But we have to remember always that the words as used by him come with a new volume of significance derived from his whole personality. Everything turns on the connotation which he gives to the term God—that is central and pivotal. What this new Kingdom of God is, or will be, he does not attempt fully to explain or analyze. In the parables, the treasure-finder and the pearl merchant achieve a great enrichment of life; so much they know at once; but what do they do with it? How do they look at it? What does it mean to them? He does not tell us. We only see that they are moving on a new plane, seeing life from a new angle, living in a fuller sense. What the new life means in its fulness, we know only when we gain the deeper knowledge of God.

He suggests that this new knowledge comes to a man from God himself—flesh and blood do not reveal it (Matt. xvi. 17). "Unto you it is given," he says on another occasion, "to know the mystery of the Kingdom of Heaven" (Mark iv. 11), and he adds that there are those who see and do not see; they are outside it; they have not the alphabet, we might say, that will open the book (*cf.* Rev. v. 3). He makes it clear at every point in the story of the Kingdom of God that there is more beyond; and he means it. It is to be a new beginning, an initiation, leading on to what we shall see but do not yet guess, though he gives us hints. We shall not easily fathom the depth of his idea of the new life, but along with it we have to study the width and boldness of his purpose. This new life is not for a few—for "the elect," in our careless phrase. He looks to a universal scope for what he is doing. It will reach far outside the bounds of Judaism. "They shall come from the east and from the west, and from the north and from the south, and shall sit down in the Kingdom of God" (Luke xiii. 29). "Wheresoever this gospel shall be preached throughout the whole world," he says (Mark xiv. 9). "My words shall not pass away" (Luke xxi. 33). All time and all existence come under his survey and are included in his plan. The range is enormous. And this was a Galilean peasant! As we gradually realize what he has in mind, must we not feel that we have not grasped anything like the full grandeur of his thought?

He makes it plain, in the second place, that it will be a matter for followers, for workers, for men who will watch and wait and dare—men with the same abandonment as himself. He calls for men to come after him, to come behind him (Mark i. 17, x. 21; Luke ix. 59). He emphasizes that they must think out the terms on which he enlists them. He does not disguise the drawbacks of his service. He calls his followers, and a very personal and individual call it is. He calls a man from the lake shore, from the nets, from the custom house.

In the third place, he clearly announces an intention to achieve something in itself of import by his death. There are those who would have us believe that his mind was obsessed with the fixed idea of his own speedy return on the clouds, and that he hurried on to death to precipitate this and the new age it was to bring. References to such a coming are indeed found in the Gospels as we have them, but we are bound to ask whence they come, and to inquire how far they represent exactly what he said; and then, if he is correctly reported, to make sure that we know exactly what he means. Those who hold this view fail to relate the texts they emphasize with others of a deeper significance, and they ignore the grandeur and penetration and depth of the man whom they make out such a dreamer. He never suggests himself that his death is to force the hand of God.

He himself is to be the doer and achiever of something. We have been apt to think of him as a great teacher, a teacher of charm and insight, or as the great example of idealism, "who saw life steadily and saw it whole." He lived, some hold, the rounded and well-poised life, the rhythmic life. No, that was Sophocles. He is greater. Here is one who penetrates far deeper into things. His treatment of the psychology of sin itself shows how much more than an example was needed. Here, as in the other chapters, but here above all we have to remember the clearness of his insight, his swiftness of penetration, his instinct for fact and reality. He means to do, to achieve, something. It is no martyr's death that he incurs. His death is a step to a purpose. "I have a baptism to be baptized with," he says (Luke xii. 50). "The Son of Man," he said, "is come to seek and to save that which was lost" (Luke xix. 10).

In discussing in the previous chapter what he meant by the term "lost," our conclusion was that for Jesus sin was far more awful, far more serious, than we commonly realize. We saw also that so profound and true a psychology of sin must imply a view of redemption at least as profound, a promise of a force more than equal to the power of sin—that "violence of habit" of which St. Augustine speaks. If the Son of Man is to save the lost, and if the lost are in danger so real, it follows that he must think of a thoroughly effective salvation, and that its achievement will be no light or easy task. "To give one's life as a ransom for many," says a modern teacher, "is of no avail, if the ransom is insufficient." What, then, and how much, does he mean by "to save," and how does he propose to do it? When the soul of man or woman has gone wrong in any of the ways discussed by Jesus—in hardness or anger, in impurity, in the refusal to treat God and his facts seriously—when the consequences that Jesus recognized have followed—what can be done to bring that soul back into effective relation with the God whom it has discarded and abandoned? That is the problem that Jesus had to face, and most of us have not thought enough about it.

First of all, how far does Jesus understand salvation to take a man? The ancient creed of the Church includes the article of belief in "the forgiveness of sins." There are those who lightly assume that this means, chiefly or solely, the remission of punishment for evil acts. This raises problems enough of itself. The whole doctrine of *Karma*, vital to Buddhism and Hinduism, is, if I understand it aright, a strong and clear warning to us that the remission of punishment is no easy matter. Not only Eastern thinkers, but Western also, insist that there is no avoidance of the consequences of action. Luther himself, using a phrase half borrowed from a Latin poet, says that forgiveness is "a knot worthy of a God's aid"—*nodus Deo vindice dignus.*[1] But in any case escape from

[1] Horace, *Ars Poetica*, 191, *Nec deus intersit nisi dignus vindice nodus Inciderit.*

the consequences of sin, when once we look on sin with the eyes of Jesus, is of relatively small importance. There are two aspects of the matter far more significant.

We have seen how Jesus regards sin as at once the cause and consequence of a degeneration of the moral nature, and as a repudiation of God. Two questions arise: Is it possible to recover lost moral quality and faculty? Is it possible for those incapacitated by sin to regain, or to enjoy, relation with God?

When we think, with Jesus, of sin first and foremost in connection with God, and take the trouble to try to give his meaning to his words, forgiveness takes on a new meaning. We have to "think like God," he says (Mark viii. 33); and perhaps God is in his thoughts neither so legal nor so biological as we are; perhaps he does not think first of edicts or of biological and psychological laws. God, according to Jesus, thinks first of his child, though of course not oblivious of his own commands and laws. Forgiveness, Jesus teaches or suggests, is primarily a question between Father and son, and he tries to lead us to believe how ready the Father is to settle that question. Once it is settled, we find, in fact, Father and son setting to work to mend the past. The evil seed has been sown and the sad crop must be reaped, the man who sowed it has to reap it—that much we all see. But Jesus hints to us that God himself loves to come in and help his reconciled son with the reaping; many hands make light work, especially when they are such hands. And even when the crop is evil in the lives of others, the most horrible outcome of sin, God is still in the field. The prodigal, when he returns, is met with a welcome, and is gradually put in possession of what he has lost—the robe, the shoes, the ring; and it all comes from his being at one with his Father again (Luke xv. 22 ff.). The Son of Man, historically, has again and again found the lost—the lost gifts, the lost faculties, the lost charms and graces—and given them back to the man whom he had also found and brought home to God.

Let us once more try to get our thoughts Theocentric as Jesus' are, and our problems become simpler, or at least fewer. God's generosity in forgiveness, God's love, he emphasizes, again and again. Will a man take Jesus at his word, and commit himself to God? That is the question. Once he will venture on this step, what pictures Jesus draws us of what happens! The son is home again; the bankruptcy, the hideous solitude, the life among animals, bestial, dirty and empty, and haunted with memories—all those things are past, when once the Father's arms are round his neck, and his kiss on his cheek. He is no more "alienated from the life of God" (Eph. iv. 18; Col. i. 21), "without God in the world" (Eph. ii. 12), an "enemy of God" (Rom. v. 10); he was lost and is found, and the Father himself, Jesus says, cries: "Let us be merry" (*Euphranthômen*). If we hesitate about it, Jesus calls us once more to "think like God," and tells us other stories, with incredible joy in them—"joy in the presence of the angels of God over one sinner that repenteth." We must go back to his central conception of God, if we are to realize what he means by salvation. St. Augustine (*Conf.*, viii. 3) brings out the value of these parables, by reminding us how much more we care for a thing that has been ours, when we have lost it and found it again. The shepherd has a new link with his sheep lost and found again, a new story of it, a shared experience; it is more his than ever. And Jesus implies that when a man is saved, he is God's again, and more God's own than ever before; and God is glad at heart. As for the man, a new power comes into his heart, and a new joy; and with God's help, in a new spirit of sunshine, he sets about mending the past in a new spirit and with a new motive—for love's sake now. If the fruit of the past is to be seen, as it constantly is, in the lives of others, he throws himself with the more energy into God's work, and when the Good Shepherd goes seeking the lost, he goes with him. Christian history bears witness, in every year of it, to what salvation means, in Jesus' sense. Punishment, consequences, crippled resources—no, he does not ask to escape them now; all as God pleases; these are not the things that matter. Life is all to be boundless love and gratitude and trust; and by and by the new man wakes up to find sin taken away, its consequences undone, the lost faculties restored, and life a fuller and richer thing than ever it was before.

Somehow so, if we read the Gospels aright, does Jesus conceive of Salvation. To achieve this for men is his purpose; and in order to do it, as we said before, his first step is to induce men to re-think God. Something must be done to touch the heart and to move the will of men, effectively; and he must do it.

With this purpose in his mind—let us weigh our words here, and reflect again upon the clearness of his insight into life and character, into moral laws, the laws of human thought and feeling, upon his profound intelligence and grasp of what moves and is real, his knowledge (a strong word to use, but we may use it) of God—with this purpose in his mind, thought out and understood, he deliberately and quietly goes to Jerusalem. He "steadfastly set his face to go to Jerusalem" (Luke ix. 51). "I must walk," he said, "to-day and to-morrow and the day following; for it cannot be that a prophet perish out of Jerusalem" (Luke xiii. 33). To Jerusalem he goes.

We may admit that with his view of the psychology of sin, he must have a serious view of redemption. But why should that involve the cross? That is our problem. But while we try to solve it, we must also remember that behind a great choice there are always more reasons than we can analyze. A man makes one of the great choices in life. What has influenced him? Ten to one, if you ask him, he does not know. Nothing else, he will say, seemed feasible; the thing was borne in on me, it came to me: reasons? He cannot tabulate reasons; the thing, he says, was so clear that I was a long way past reasons. And yet he was right; he had reasons enough. What parent ever analyzed reasons for loving his children, or would tabulate them for you? Jesus does not explain his reasons. We find, I think, that we are apt to have far more reasons for doing what we know is wrong, than we have for doing what we know is right. We do not want reasons for doing what is right; we know it is right, and there is an end of it. Once again, Jesus, with his clear eye for the real, sees what he must do. The salvation of the lost means the cross for himself. But why? we ask again. We must look a little closer if we are to understand him. We shall not easily understand him in all his thoughts, but part of our education comes from the endeavor to follow him here, to "be with him," in the phrase with which we began.

First of all we may put his love of men. He never lost the individual in the mass, never lost sight of the human being who needed God. The teacher who put the law of kindness in the great phrase, "Go with him twain" (Matt. v. 41), was not likely to limit himself in meeting men's needs. He was bound to do more than we should expect, when he saw people whom he could help; and it is that spirit of abounding generosity that shows a man what to do (Luke vi. 38). Everywhere, every day, he met the call that quickened thought and shaped purpose.

He walked down a street; and the scene of misery or of sin came upon him with pressure; he could not pass by, as we do, and fail to note what we do not wish to think of. He knows a pressure upon his spirit for the man, the child, the woman—for the one who sins, the one who suffers, the other who dies. They must be got in touch with God. He sits with his disciples at a meal—the men whom he loved—he watches them, he listens to them. Peter, James, John, one after the other, becomes a call to him. They need redemption; they need far more than they dream; they need God. That pressure is there night and day—it becomes intercession, and that grows into inspiration. Our prayers suffer, some one has said, for our want of our identification with the world's sin and misery. He was identified with the world's sin and misery, and they followed him into his prayer. It becomes with him an imperative necessity to effect man's reconciliation with God. All his experience of man, his love of man, call him that way.

The second great momentum comes from the love of God, and his faith in God. Here, again, we must emphasize for ourselves his criticism of Peter: "You think like a man and not like God" (Mark viii. 33). We do not see God, as Jesus did. He must make plain to men, as it never was made plain before, the love of God. He must secure that it is for every man the greatest reality in the world, the one great flaming fact that burns itself living into every man's consciousness. He sees that for this God calls him to the cross, so much so that when he prays in the garden that the cup may pass, his thoughts range back to "Thy will" (Matt. xxvi. 42). It is God's Will. Even if he does not himself see all involved, still God knows the reason; God will manage; God wishes it. "Have faith in God," he used to say (Mark xi. 22). This faith which he has in God is one of the things that take him to the cross.

In the third place, we must not forget his sense of his own peculiar relation to God. If it is safe to rely on St. Mark's chronological date here, he does not speak of this until Peter has called him the Messiah. He accepts the title (Mark viii. 29). He also uses the description, Son of Man, with its suggestions from the past. He forgives sins. He speaks throughout the Gospels as one apart, as one distinct from us, closely as he is identified with us—and all this from a son of fact, who is not insane, who is not a quack, whose eyes are wide open for the real; whose instinct for the ultimate truth is so keen; who lives face to face with God. What does it mean? This, for one thing, that most of us have not given attention enough to this matter. I have confined myself in these chapters to the Synoptic Gospels, with only two or three references to the Fourth Gospel, and on the evidence of the Synoptic Gospels, taken by themselves, it is clear that he means a great deal more than we have cared to examine. He is the great interpreter of God, and it is borne in upon him that only by the cross can he interpret God, make God real to us, and bring us to the very heart of God. That is his purpose.

The cross is the outcome of his deepest mind, of his prayer life. It is more like him than anything else he ever did. It has in it more of him. Whoever he was, whoever he is, whatever our Christology, one fact stands out. It was his love of men and women and his faith in God that took him there.

Was he justified? was he right? or was it a delusion?

First of all, let us go back to a historic event. The resurrection is, to a historian, not very clear in its details. But is it the detail or the central fact that matters? Take away the resurrection, however it happened, whatever it was, and the history of the Church is unintelligible. We live in a rational world—a world, that is, where, however much remains as yet unexplained, everything has a promise of being lucid, everything has reason in it. Great results have great causes. We have to find, somewhere or other, between the crucifixion and the first preaching of the disciples in Jerusalem, something that entirely changed the character of that group of men.

Something happened, so tremendous and so vital, that it changed not only the character of the movement and the men—but with them the whole history of the world. The evidence for the resurrection is not so much what we read in the Gospels as what we find in the rest of the New Testament—the new life of the disciples. They are a new group. When it came to the cross, his cross, they ran away. A few weeks later we find them rejoicing to be beaten, imprisoned and put to death (Acts v. 41). What had happened? What we have to explain is a new life—a new life of prayer and joy and power, a new indifference to physical death, in a new relation to God. That is one outcome of the cross and of what followed; and as historians we have to explain it. We have also to explain how the disciples came to conceive of another Galilean—a carpenter whom they might have seen sawing and sweating in his shop, with whom they tramped the roads of Palestine, whom they saw done to death in ignominy and derision—sitting at the right hand of God. Taken by itself, we might call such a belief mere folly; but too much goes with it for so easy an explanation. The cross was not the end. As Mr. Neville Talbot has recently pointed out in his book, "The Mind of the Disciples," if the story stopped with the cross, God remains unexplained, and the story ends in unrelieved tragedy. But it does not end in tragedy; it ends—if we can use the word as yet—in joy and faith and victory; and these—how should we have seen them but for the cross? They are bound up with his choice of the cross and his triumph over it all. Death is not what it was—"the last line of all," as Horace says. Life and immortality have been brought to light (2 Tim. i. 10). "The Lamb of God taketh away the sin of the world." So we read at the beginning of the Fourth Gospel, and the historical critic may tell us that he does not think that John the Baptist said it. None the less, it is a wonderful summary of what Jesus has done, especially wonderful if we think of it being written fifty or sixty years after the crucifixion. For, as we survey the centuries, we find that the Lamb of God has taken away the sin of the world—to a degree that no one can imagine who has not studied the ancient world. Those who know the heathen world intimately will know best the difference he has made. All this new life, this new joy, this new victory over death and sin is attached to the living and victorious Son of God. The task of Paul and the others is, as Dr. Cairns says, "re-thinking everything in the terms of the resurrection." It is the new factor in the problem of God, so to speak—the new factor which alters everything that relates to God. That is saying a great deal, but when we look at Christian history, is it saying too much?

But still our first question is unanswered; why should it have been the cross? One thinker of our day has suggested that, after all, suffering is a language intelligible to the very simplest, while its meaning is not exhausted by the deepest. The problem of pain is always with us. And he chose pain. He never said that pain is a good thing; he cured it. But he chose it. The ancient world stumbled on that very thing. God and a Godlike man, their philosophers said, are not susceptible to pain, to suffering. That was an axiom, very little challenged. Then if Jesus suffered, he was not God; if he was God, he did not suffer. The Church denied that, just as the Church to-day rejects another hasty antithesis about pain, that comes from New England. He chose pain, and he knew what he was choosing. Then let us be in no hurry about refusing it, but let us look into it. He chose it—that is the greatest fact known to us about pain.

Again, the death of Christ reveals sin in its real significance, in its true perspective, outside the realm of accident and among the deepest things of God, *sub specie æternitatis*. Men count themselves very decent people; so thought the priests and the Pharisees, and they were.

There is nothing about them that one cannot find in most religious communities and in all governing classes: the sense of the value of themselves, their preconceptions and their judgments—a strong feeling of the importance of the work they have to do, along with a certain reluctance to face strange facts, and some indifference as to what happens to other people if the accepted theory of the Cause or the State require them to suffer. There is nothing about Pilate and Herod, and the Pharisees and the priests, that is very different from ourselves. But how it looks in front of the cross! We begin to see how it looks in the sight of God, and that alters everything; it upsets all our standards, and teaches us a new self-criticism.

"You think like man, and not like God," said Jesus (Mark viii. 33). The cross reveals God most sympathetically. We see God in the light of the fullest and profoundest and tenderest revelation that the world has had. "My God, my God, why hast thou forsaken me?" that is the cry of Jesus on the cross. I have sometimes thought there never was an utterance that reveals more amazingly the distance between feeling and fact. That was how he felt—worn out, betrayed, spat upon, rejected. We feel that God was more there than ever. As has been said, if it is not God, it is nothing. "God," says Paul, "was in Christ, reconciling the world unto himself" (2 Cor. v. 19). He chose the cross; and in choosing it, Christians have always felt, he revealed God; and that is the center of the great act of Redemption.

But there is a condition antecedent to understanding the cross. We have, as we agreed, to ask ourselves, what is the experience which led him to think as he did? In the simpler language of the Gospels, quite plain and easy to understand, the call to follow comes first—the call to deeper association with Jesus Christ in his love for men. Do not our consciences tell us that, if we really loved people as Jesus does, if we understood them as sympathetically and cared as much for them, the cross would be far more intelligible to us? But if, in plain fact, we do not see why we should bear the cross for others, why we should deny and obliterate self on this scale for the salvation of men—how, I ask, to people of such a mind should Jesus be intelligible? It is not to be expected. In no other sphere would one dream of it. When a man avows that he does not care for art or poetry, who would wish to show him poem or picture? How should a person, who does not care for men, understand the cross? Deeper association, then, with Jesus in his love of men, in his agony, in his trust in God—that is the key to all. As we agreed at the very beginning, we have to know him before we can understand him.

It all depends in the long run on one thing; and that we find in the verse with which we started: "And as they followed, they began to be afraid." But they followed. We can understand their fear. It comes to a man in this way. If Jesus crucified means anything like what the Church has said, and has believed; if God is in that man of Nazareth reconciling the world to Himself; if there is real meaning in the Incarnation at all; if all this language represents fact; "then," he may say, "I am wholly at a loss about everything else." A man builds up a world of thought for himself—we all do—a scheme of things; and to a man with a thought-out view of the world, it may come with an enormous shock to realize this incredible idea, this incredible truth, of God in Christ. Those who have dwelt most on it, and value it most, may be most apt to understand what I mean by calling it incredible. Think of it. It takes your breath away. If that is true, does not the whole plan of my life fall to pieces—my whole scheme of things for the world, my whole body of intellectual conceptions? And the man to whom this happens may well say he is afraid. He is afraid, because it is so strange; because, when you realize it, it takes you into a new world; you cannot grasp it. A man whose instinct is for truth may hesitate—will hesitate—about a conception like this. "Is it possible," he will ask himself, "that I am deluded?" And another thought rises up again and again, "Where will it take me?" We can understand a man being afraid in that way. I do not think we have much right *not* to be afraid. If it is the incarnation of God, what right have we not to be afraid? Then, of course, a man will say that to follow Christ involves too much in the way of sacrifice. He is afraid on lower grounds, afraid of his family, afraid for his career; he hesitates. To that man the thing will be unintelligible. The experience of St. Augustine, revealed in his *Confessions*, is illuminative here. He had intellectual difficulties in his approach to the Christian position, but the rate of progress became materially quicker when he realized that the moral difficulties came first, that a practical step had to be taken. So with us—to decide the issue, how far are we prepared to go with Jesus? Have we realized the experience behind his thought? The rule which we laid down at the beginning holds. How far are we prepared to go in sharing that experience? That will measure our right to understand him. Once again, in the plainest language, are we prepared to follow, as the disciples followed, afraid as they were?

Where is he going? Where is he taking them? They wonder; they do not know; they are uneasy. But when all is said, the figure on the road ahead of them, waiting for them now and looking round, is the Jesus who loves them and whom they love.

And one can imagine the feeling rising in the mind of one and another of them: "I don't know where he is going, or where he is taking us, but I must be with him." There we reach again what the whole story began with—he chose twelve that they might "be with him." To understand him, we, too, must be with him. What takes men there? After all, it is, in the familiar phrase, the love of Jesus. If one loves the leader, it is easier to follow him. But, whether you understand him or whether you don't, if you love him you are glad that he chose the cross, and you are glad that you are one of his people.

CHAPTER IX

THE CHRISTIAN CHURCH IN THE ROMAN EMPIRE

IMPERIAL Rome governed the whole of the Mediterranean world—a larger proportion and a greater variety of the human race than has ever been under one government. So far as numbers go, the Russian Empire to-day, the Chinese and the British, each far exceed it; for the population of the world is vastly larger than it was in Rome's days. But there was a peculiar unity about the Roman Empire, for it embraced, as men thought, all civilized mankind. It was known that, far away in the East, there were people called Indians, who had fought with Alexander the Great, but there was little real knowledge of them. Beyond India, there were vague rumors of a land where silk grew on the leaves of the trees. But civilized mankind was under the control of Rome. It was one rule of many races, many kingdoms, princedoms, cities, cantons, and tribes—a wise rule, a rule that allowed the maximum of local government and traditional usage. Rome not merely conquered but captured men all over the world; ruled them, as a poet said, like a mother, not a queen, and bound them to herself. Men were eager, not so much to shake off her yoke, as to be Romans; and from the Atlantic to the Euphrates men, not of Roman blood, were proud to bear Roman names and to be Roman citizens. "I was free born," said St. Paul, not without a touch of satisfaction (Acts xxii. 25-28). A general peace prevailed through the Roman world—a peace that was new to mankind. There was freedom of intercourse; one of the boasts made by the writers of the Roman Empire is of this new freedom to travel, to go anywhere one pleased. Piracy on the sea, brigandage on the land, had been put down, and there was a very great deal of travel. The Roman became an inveterate tourist. He went to the famous scenes of Asia Minor, to Troy above all—to "sunny Rhodes and Mitylene"—to Egypt. Merchants went everywhere. And there was a fusing of cultures, traditions, and creeds, all over the Mediterranean world. Centuries before, Alexander the Great had struck out the splendid idea of the marriage of East and West. He secured it by breaking down the Persian Empire, and making one Empire from the Adriatic to this side of the Sutlej or Bias. He desired to cement this marriage of East and West in a way of his own. He took three hundred captive princesses and ladies, and married them in a batch to Macedonian officers—a very characteristic piece of symbolism. But his idea was greater and truer than the symbol.

The Roman marriage of the East and West was a more real thing, for behind it lay three centuries of growing intercourse and knowledge along Alexander's lines. In the sphere of religion we find it most clearly. There rises a resultant world-religion—a religion that embraces all the cults, all the creeds, and at last all the philosophies, in one great system. That religion held the world. It is true, there were exceptions. There was a small and objectionable race called Jews; there were possibly some Druids in Southern Britain; and here and there was a solitary atheist who represented no one but himself. These few exceptions were the freaks amongst mankind.

Apart from them mankind was united in its general beliefs about the gods. The world had one religion.

First of all, let us try to estimate the strength of this old Mediterranean Paganism. It was strong in its great traditions. Plutarch, who lived from about 50 A.D. to 117 or so, is our great exponent of this old religion. To him I shall have to refer constantly. He was a writer of charm, a man with many gifts. Plutarch's *Lives* was the great staple of education in the Renaissance—and as good a one, perhaps, as we have yet discovered, even in this age when there are so many theories of education with foreign names. Plutarch, then, writing about Delphi, the shrine and oracle of the god Apollo, said that men had been "in anguish and fear lest Delphi should lose its glory of three thousand years"—and Delphi has not lost it. For ninety generations the god has been giving oracles to the Greek world, to private people, to kings, to cities, to nations—and on all sorts of subjects, on the foundation of colonies, the declaration of wars, personal guidance and the hope of heirs. You may test the god where you will, Plutarch claimed, you will not find an instance of a false oracle. Readers of Greek history will remember another great writer of as much charm, five hundred years before, Herodotus, who was not so sure about all the oracles. But let us think what it means,—to look back over three thousand years of one faith, unbroken. Egyptian religion had been unchallenged for longer still, even if we allow Plutarch's three thousand years. The oldest remains in Egypt antedate, we are told, 4000 B.C., and all through history, with the exception of the solitary reign of Amen-Hotep III., Egypt worshiped the same gods, with additions, as time went on. Again an unbroken tradition. And how long, under various names, had Cybele, Mother of Gods, been worshiped in Asia? By our era all these religions were fused into one religion, of many cults and rites and ancient traditions; and the incredible weight of old tradition in that world is hard to overestimate.

The old religion was strong in the splendor of its art and its architecture. The severe, beautiful lines of the Greek temple are familiar to us still; and, until I saw the Taj, I think I should have doubted whether there could be anything more beautiful. Architecture was consecrated to the gods, and so was art. You go to Delphi, said Plutarch, and see those wonderful works of the ancient artists and sculptors, as fresh still as if they had left the chisel yesterday, and they had stood there for hundreds of years, wonderful in their beauty. Think of some of the remains of the Greek art—of that Victory, for instance, which the Messenians set on the temple at Olympia in 421 B.C. She stood on a block of stone on the temple, but the block was painted blue, so that, as the spectator came up, he saw the temple and the angle of its roof, and then a gap of blue sky and the goddess just alighting on the summit of the temple. From what is left of her, broken and headless, but still beautiful, we can picture her flying through the air—the wind has blown her dress back against her, and you see its folds freshly caught by the breeze. And all this the artist had disentangled from a rough block of stone—so vivid was his conception of the goddess, and so sure his hand. There are those who say that the conventional picture of God of the great artists is moulded after the Zeus of Pheidias. Egypt again had other portrayals of the gods—on a pattern of her own, strange and massive and huge, far older. About six hundred years before

Christ the Egyptian King, Psammetichos (Psem Tek), hired Greek soldiers and marched them hundreds of miles up the Nile. The Greek soldiers, one idle day, carved their names on the legs of the colossal gods seated at Abu Symbel. Their names are found there to-day. So old are these gods.

The religion was strong in the splendor of its ceremony. Every year the Athenian people went to Eleusis in splendid procession to worship, to be initiated into the rites of the Earth-Mother and her virgin daughter, who had taught men the use of grain and the arts of farming—rites linked with an immemorial past, awful rites that gave men a new hope of eternal life. The Mother of the Gods, from Phrygia in Asia Minor, had her rites, too; and her cult spread all over the world. When the Roman poet, Lucretius, wants to describe the wonder and magic of the pageant of Nature in the spring-time he goes to the pomp of Cybele. The nearest thing to it which we can imagine is Botticelli's picture of the Triumph of Spring. Lucretius was a poet to whom the gods were idle and irrelevant; yet to that pageant he goes for a picture of the miraculous life of nature. More splendid still were the rites of the Egyptian Isis, celebrated all over the world. Her priests, shaven and linen-clad, carried symbols of an unguessed antiquity and magical power. They launched a boat with a flame upon it—on the river in Egypt, on the sea in Greece. All these cults made deep impressions on the worshipers, as our records tell us. The appeal of religious emotion was noticed by Aristotle, who remarked, however, that it was rather feeling than intellect that was touched—a shrewd criticism that deserves to be remembered still.

The gods were strong in their actual manifestations of themselves. Apollo for ninety generations had spoken in Delphi. At Epidauros there was a shrine of Asclepios. Its monuments have been collected and edited by Dr. Caton of Liverpool. There sick men and women came, lived a quiet life of diet and religious ceremony, preparing for the night on which they should sleep in the temple. On that night the god came to them, they said, in that mood or state where they lay "between asleep and awake, sometimes as in a dream and then as in a waking vision—one's hair stood on end, but one shed tears of joy and felt light-hearted." Others said they definitely saw him. He came and told them what to do; on waking they did it and were healed; or he touched them then and there, and cured them as they lay. Some of the cures recorded on the monuments are perhaps strange to our ideas of medicine. One records how the god came to man dreadfully afflicted with dropsy, cut off his head, turned him upside down and let the fluid run out, and then replaced his head with a neat join. Some modern readers may doubt this story; but that the god did heal people, men firmly believed. We, too, may believe that people were healed, perhaps by living a healthy life in a quiet place, a life of regimen and diet; and perhaps faith-healing or suggestion played as strong a part as anything else. Even the Christians believed that these gods had a certain power; they were evil spirits.

Not only the gods of the temples would manifest themselves of their grace. Every man had a guardian spirit, a *genius*; and by proper means he could be "compelled" to show himself visibly. The pupils of Plotinus conjured up his *genius*, and it came—not a dæmon, but a god. The right formula (*mantram*) and the right stone in the hand—and a man had a wonderful power over the gods themselves. This was called *theurgy*.

But the great strength of this old religion was its infinite adaptability. It made peace with every god and goddess that it met. It adopted them all. As a French scholar has said, where there is polytheism there are no false gods. All the religions were fused and the gods were blended. The Roman went to Greece and identified Jupiter with Zeus; he went to Egypt and found him in Amun (Ammon); he went to Syria and found him in Baal. If the Jew had not been so foolish and awkward, there might have been a Jupiter Jehovah as well. It was a catholic faith, embracing everything—cult and creed and philosophy—strong in all the ways we have surveyed and in many more, above all because it was unchallenged.

And yet, where is that religion to-day? That, to me, is one of the most significant questions in history—more so, the longer I stay in India. Men *knew* that that religion of Greece and Rome was eternal; yet it is utterly gone. Why? How *could* it go? What conceivable power was there, I do not say, to bring it down, but to abolish it so thoroughly, that not a soul in Egypt worships Isis—how many even know her name?—not a soul in Italy thinks of Jove but as a fancy, and Pallas Athene in Athens itself is a mere memory? That is the problem, the historical problem, with which we have now to deal.

First of all, let us look again, and more closely, at that old religion—we shall find in it at least four cardinal weaknesses.

First, it stands for "the unexamined life," as Plato called it. "The unexamined life," he says, "is not livable for a human being." A man, who is a man, must cross-examine life, must make life face up to him and yield its secrets. He must know what it means, the significance of every relation of life—father and child, man and wife, citizen and city, subject and king, man and the world—above all, man and God. We must examine and know. But this old religion stood by tradition and not reflection. There was no deep sense of truth. Plutarch admired his father, and he describes, with warm approval, how his father once said to a man: "That is a dangerous question, not to be discussed at all—when you question the opinion we hold about the gods, and ask reason and demonstration for everything." Such an attitude means mistrust, it means at bottom a fundamental unfaith. The house is beautiful; do not touch it; it is riddled by white ants, by dry rot, and it would fall. That is not faith; it is a strange confession; but all who hesitate at changes, I think, make that confession sooner or later. There is a line of Kabir which puts the essence of this: "Penance is not equal to truth, nor is there any sin like untruth." This was one of the essential weaknesses of that old religion—its fear, and the absence of a deep sense of truth.

In the next place, there is no real association of morals with religion. The old stories were full of the adventures of Jupiter, or Zeus, with the heroines, mortal women, whom he loved. Of some 1900 wall paintings at Pompeii, examined by a German scholar and antiquary, some 1400 represent mythological subjects, largely the stories of the loves of Jupiter. The Latin dramatist Terence pictures the young man looking at one of these paintings and saying to himself, "If Jupiter did it, why should not I?" Centuries later we find Augustine quoting that sentence.

It has been said that few things tended more strongly against morality than the stories of the gods preserved by Homer and Hesiod. Plato loved Homer; so much the more striking is his resolve that in his *Republic* there should be no Homer. Men said: "Ah, but you don't understand; those stories are allegories. They do not mean what they say; they mean something deeper." But Plato said we must speak of God always as he is; we must in no case tell lies about God "*whether they are allegories or whether they are not allegories.*" Plato, like every real thinker, sees that this pretence of allegory is a sham. The story did its mischief whether it was allegory or not; it stood between man and God, and headed men on to wrong lines, turned men away from the moral standard.

There was more. Every year, as we saw, men went to be initiated into the rites of Demeter at Eleusis, a few miles from Athens. And we read how one of the great Athenian orators, Lysias, went there and took with him to be initiated a harlot, with whom he was living, and the woman's proprietress—a squalid party; and they were initiated. Their morals made no difference; the priests and the goddesses offered no objection. In the temple of Aphrodite at Corinth there were women slaves dedicated to the goddess, who owned them, and who received the wages of their shame. With what voice could religion speak for morality in Corinth? At Comana in Syria—we read in Strabo the geographer, about the time of Christ—there was a temple where there were a thousand of these temple slaves. I say again, that is the unexamined life. God and goddess have nothing to say about some of the most sacred relations in life. God, goddess, priest, worshiper, never gave a thought to these poor creatures, dedicated, not by themselves, to this awful life —human natures with the craving of the real woman for husband and child, for the love of home, but never to know it. That was associated with religion; that was religion. There was always a minimum of protest from the Greek temples against wrong or for right. It is remarked, again and again, that all the great lessons came, not from the temples, not from the priests, but from the poets and philosophers, from the thinkers in revolt against the religion of their people. Curiously enough, even in Homer himself, it is plain that the heroes, the men, are on a higher moral plane than the gods; and all through Greek history the gods are a drag on morality. What a weakness in religion! The sense of wrong and right is innate in man; it may be undeveloped, or it may be deadened, but it is instinctive; and a religion which does not know it, or which finds the difference between right and wrong to lie in matters of taboo or ceremonial defilement, cannot speak to one of the deepest needs of the human heart, the need of forgiveness. There is no righteousness, in the long run, about these gods.

In the third place, the religion has the common weakness of all polytheism. Men were afraid of the gods; there were thousands and thousands, hosts of them. At every turn you ran into one, a new one; you could never be certain that you would not offend some unknown god or goddess. Superstition was the curse of the day. You had to make peace with all these gods and goddesses—and not with them alone. For there was another class of supernatural beings, dangerous if unpropitiated, the dæmons, the spirits that inhabited the air, that presided over life and its stages, that helped or hated the human soul, spiteful and evil half-divine beings, that sent illness, bad luck, madness, that stole the honors of the gods themselves and insisted on rituals and worship, often unclean, often cruel, but inevitable. A man must watch himself closely if he was to be safe from them all, if he was to keep wife and child and home safe.

Superstition, men said, was the one curse of life that made no truce with sleep. A famous Christian writer of the second century, Tatian, speaks of the enormous relief that he found in getting away from the tyranny of ten thousand gods to be under a monarchy of One. A modern Japanese, Uchimura, said the same thing: "One God, not eight millions; that was joyful news to me."

Fourth, this religion took from the grave none of its terrors. There might be a world beyond, and there might not. At any rate, "be initiated," said the priests; "you will have to pay us something, but it is worth it." Prophets and quacks, said Plato, came to rich men's doors and made them believe that they could rid them of all alarm for the next world, by incantations and charms and other things, by a series of feasts and jollifications. So they said, and men did what they were told; but it did not take away the fear of death.

From the first century onwards men began systematically to defend this old paganism. Plutarch wrote a series of books in its behalf. He brings in something like love of god for man. He speaks of "the friendly Apollo." But the weakness of Plutarch as an apologist is his weakness as biographer—he never really gets at the bottom of anything. In biography he gives us the characteristic rather than the character. Here he never faces the real issue. It is all defence, apology, ingenuity; but he defends far too much. He admits there are obscene rites; there had been human sacrifices; but the gods cannot have ordained them; dæmons, who stole the names of gods, imposed these on men—not the gods; men practiced them to avert the anger of dæmons. The gods are good. Waiving the fact that he had not much evidence for this in the mythology, how was a man to distinguish god from dæmon, to know which is which? He does not tell us. Again he speaks of the image of Osiris with three *lingams*. He apologizes for it; he defends it; for the triplicity is a symbol of godhead, and it means that God is the origin of all life. Yes, but what that religion needed was a great reformer, who should have cut the religion clear adrift from idols of every kind, from the old mythology, from obscenity. It may very well be that such a reformer was unthinkable; even if he had appeared, he would have been foredoomed to fail, as the compromise of the Stoics shows. Plutarch and his kind did not attempt this. They loved the past and the old ways. At heart they were afraid of the gods and were afraid of tradition. Culture and charm will do a great deal, but they do not suffice for a religion—either to make one or to redeem it.

The Stoics reached, I think, the highest moral level in that Roman world—great men, great teachers of morals, great characters; but as for the crowd, they said, let them go on in the religions of their own cities; what they had learnt from their fathers, let them do. So much for the ignorant; for us, of course, something else. That seems to be a fundamentally wrong defense of religion. It gets the proportions wrong. It means that we, who are people of culture, are a great deal nearer to God than the crowd. But if we realize God at all, we feel that we are none of us very far apart down here. The most brilliant men are amenable to the temptations of the savage and of the dock laborer. There was a further danger, little noticed at first, that life is apt to be overborne by the vulgar, the ignorant, if there is not a steady campaign to enlighten every man. The Roman house was full of slaves; they taught the children—taught them about gods and goddesses, from Syria, from Egypt, and kept thought and life and morals on a low plane. An ignorant public is an unspeakable danger everywhere, but especially in religion.

The last great system of defence was the New Platonism. It had not very much to do with Plato, except that it read him and quoted him as a great authority. The Neo-Platonists did not face facts as Plato did. They lived on quotations, on authority and fancy, great thinkers as some of them were. They pictured the universe as one vast unity. Far beyond all things is God. Of God man can form no conception. Think, they would say, of all the exalted and wonderful and beautiful concepts you can imagine; then deny them. God is beyond. God is beyond being; you can conceive of being, and therefore to predicate being of God is to limit him. You cannot think of God; for, if you could think of God, God would be in relation with you; God is insusceptible of relation with man. He neither wills, nor thinks of man, nor can man think of him. A modern philosopher has summed up their God as the deification of the word "not." This God, then, who is not, willed—no! not "willed"; he could not will; but whether he willed or did not will, in some way or other there was an emanation; not God, but very much of God; very divine, but not all God; from this another and another in a descending series, down to the dæmons, and down to men. All that is, is God; evil is not-being. One of the great features of the system was that it guaranteed all the old religions—for the crowd; while for the initiated, for the esoteric, it had something more—it had mystic trance, mystic vision, mystic comprehension. Twice or three times, Plotinus, by a great leap away from all mortal things, saw God. In the meantime, the philosophy justified all the old rites.

Side by side with this great defense were what are known as the Christian heresies. They are not exactly Christian. Groups of people endeavored to combine Christianity with the old thought, with philosophy, theosophy, theurgy, and magic. They were eclectics; they compromised. The German thinker, Novalis, said very justly that all eclectics are sceptics, and the more eclectic the more sceptic. These mixtures could not prevail.

But religions have, historically, a wonderful way of living in spite of their weaknesses—yes, and in spite of their apologetics. A religion may be stained with all sorts of evil, and may communicate it; and yet it will survive, until there is an alternative with more truth and more dynamic. The old paganism outlived Plato's criticisms and Plutarch's defenses. For the great masses of people neither might have written.

Into this world came the Christian Church. I have tried to draw the picture of the great pagan religion, with its enormous strength, its universal acceptance, its great traditions, its splendors of art and ceremony, its manifest proofs of its gods—everything that, to the ordinary mind, could make for reality and for power; to show how absolutely inconceivable it was that it could ever pass away.

Then comes the Christian Church—a ludicrous collection of trivial people, very ignorant and very common; fishermen and publicans, as the Gospels show us, "the baker and the fuller," as Celsus said with a sneer. Yes, and every kind of unclean and disreputable person they urged to join them, quite unlike all decent and established religions. And they took the children and women of the family away into a corner, and whispered to them and misled them—"Only believe!" was their one great word. The whole thing was incredibly silly. Paul went to Athens, and they asked him there about his religion; and when he spoke to them about Jesus rising from the dead, they sniggered, and the more polite suggested "another day." Everybody knew that dead men do not rise. It was a silly religion. Celsus pictured the frogs in symposium round a swamp, croaking to one another how God forsakes the whole universe, the spheres of heaven, to dwell with *us;* we frogs are so like God; he never ceases to seek how we may dwell with him for ever; but some of us are sinners, so God will come—or send his son—and burn them up; and the rest of us will live with him for eternity. Is not that very like the Christian religion? Celsus asked. It has been replied that, if the frogs really could say this and did say this, then their statement might be quite reasonable. But our main purpose for the moment is to realize the utterly inconceivable absurdity of this bunch of Galilean fishermen—and fools and rascals and maniacs—setting out to capture the world. One of them wrote an Apocalypse. He was in a penal settlement on Patmos, when he wrote it. The sect was in a fair way of being stamped out in blood, as a matter of fact; but this dreamer saw a triumphant Church of ten thousand times ten thousand—and thousands of thousands—there were hardly as many people in the world at that time; the great Rome had fallen and the "Lamb" ruled. Imagine the amusement of a Roman pagan of 100 A.D. who read the absurd book. Yet the dream has come true; that Church has triumphed. Where is the old religion? Christ has conquered, and all the gods have gone, utterly gone—they are memories now, and nothing more.

Why did they go? The Christian Church refused to compromise.

A pagan could have seen no real reason why Jesus should not be a demi-god like Herakles or Dionysos; no reason, either, why a man should not worship Jesus as well as these. One of the Roman Emperors, a little after 200 A.D., had in his private sanctuary four or five statues of gods, and one of them was Jesus. Why not? The Roman world had open arms for Jesus as well as any other god or demi-god, if people would be sensible; but the Christian said, No. He would not allow Jesus to be put into that pantheon, nor would he worship the gods himself, not even the *genius* of the Emperor, his guardian spirit. The Christian proclaimed a war of religion in which there shall be no compromise and no peace, till Christ is lord of all; the thing shall be fought out to the bitter end. And it has been. He was resolved that the old gods should go; and they have gone. How was it done?

Here we touch what I think one of the greatest wonders that history has to show. How did the Church do it? If I may invent or adapt three words, the Christian "out-lived" the pagan, "out-died" him, and "out-thought" him. He came into the world and lived a great deal better than the pagan; he beat him hollow in living. Paul's Epistles to the Corinthians do not indicate a high standard of life at Corinth. The Corinthians were a very poor sort of Christians. But another Epistle, written to the Corinthians a generation later, speaks of their passion for being kind to men, and of a broadened and deeper life, in spite of their weaknesses. Here and there one recognizes failure all along the line—yes, but the line advances.

The old world had had morals, plenty of morals—the Stoics overflowed with morals. But the Christian came into the world, not with a system of morality—he had rules, indeed—"which," asks Tertullian, "is the ampler rule, Thou shalt not commit adultery, or the rule that forbids a single lustful look?"—but it was not rules so much that he brought into the world as a great passion. "The Son of God," he said, "loved me and gave himself for me. That man—Jesus Christ loved him, gave himself for him. He is the friend of my best Friend. My best Friend loves that man, gave himself for him, died for him." How it alters all the relations of life! Who can kill or rob another man, when he remembers whose hands were nailed to the Cross for that man? See how it bears on another side of morality. Tertullian strikes out a great phrase, a new idea altogether, when he speaks of "the victim of the common lust." Christ died for her—how it safeguards her and uplifts her! Men came into the world full of this passion for Jesus Christ. They went to the slave and to the temple-woman and told them: "The Son of God loved you and gave himself for you"; and they believed it, and rose into a new life. To be redeemed by the Son of God gave the slave a new self-respect, a new manhood. He astonished people by his truth, his honesty, his cleanness; and there was a new brightness and gaiety about him. So there was about the woman. They sang, they overflowed with good temper. It seemed as if they had been born again. As Clement of Rome wrote, the Holy Spirit was a glad spirit. The word used both by him and by St. Augustine is that which gives us the English word "hilarious." There was a new gladness and happiness about these people. "It befits Truth to laugh, because she is glad—to play with her rivals because she is free from fear," so said Tertullian. Of course, there were those who broke down, but Julian the Apostate, in his letters to his heathen priests, is a reluctant witness to the higher character of Christian life. And it was Jesus who was the secret of it.

The pagan noticed the new fortitude in the face of death. Tertullian himself was immensely impressed with it. He had never troubled to look at the Gospels. Nobody bothered to read them unless they were converted already, he said. But he seems to have seen these Christian martyrs die. "Every man," he said, "who sees it, is moved with some misgiving, and is set on fire to learn the reason; he inquires and he is taught; and when he has learnt the truth, he instantly follows it himself as well." "No one would have wished to be killed, unless he was in possession of the truth." I think that is autobiography. The intellectual energy of the man is worth noting—his insistence on understanding, his instant resolution; such qualities, we saw, had won the admiration of Jesus. Here is a man who sacrifices a great career—his genius, his wit, his humor, fire, power, learning, philosophy, everything thrown at Christ's feet, and Christ uses them all.

Then came a day when persecution was breaking out again. Some Christians were for "fleeing to the next city"—it was the one text in their Bible, he said. He said: "I stay here." Any day the mob might get excited and shout: "The Christians to the lions." They knew the street in which he lived, and they would drag him—the scholar, the man of letters and of imagination—naked through the streets; torn and bleeding, they would tie him to the stake in the middle of the amphitheater and pile faggots round him, and there he would stand waiting to be burnt alive; or, it might be, to be killed by the beasts. Any hour, any day. "I stay here," he said. What does it cost a man to do that? People asked what was the magic of it. The magic of it was just this—on the other side of the fire was the same Friend; "if he wants me to be burnt alive, I am here." Jesus Christ was the secret of it.

The Christians out-thought the pagan world. How could they fail to? "We have peace with God," said Paul. They moved about in a new world, which was their Father's world. They would go to the shrines and ask uncomfortable questions. Lucian, who was a pagan and a scoffer, said that on one side of the shrines the notice was posted: "Christians outside." The Christians saw too much. The living god in that shrine was a big snake with a mask tied on—good enough for the pagan; but the Christian would see the strings. Even the dæmons they dismissed to irrelevance and non-entity. The essence of magic was to be able to link the name of a dæmon with the name of one's enemy, to set the dæmon on the man. "Very well," said the Christian, "link my name with your dæmons. Use my name in any magic you like.

There is a name that is above every name; I am not afraid." That put the dæmons into their right place, and by and by they vanished, dropped out, died of sheer inanition and neglect. Wherever Jesus Christ has been, the dæmons have gone. "There used to be fairies," said an old woman in the Highlands of Scotland to a friend of mine, "but the Gospel came and drove them away." I do not know what is going to keep them away yet but Jesus Christ. The Christian read the ancient literature with the same freedom of mind, and was not in bondage to it; he had a new outlook; he could criticise more freely. One great principle is given by Clement of Alexandria: "The beautiful, wherever it is, is ours, because it came from our God." The Christian read the best books, assimilated them, and lived the freest intellectual life that the world had. Jesus had set him to be true to fact. Why had Christian churches to be so much larger than pagan temples? Why are they so still? Because the sermon is in the very center of all Christian worship—clear, definite Christian teaching about Jesus Christ. There is no place for an ignorant Christian. From the very start every Christian had to know and to understand, and he had to read the Gospels; he had to be able to give the reason for his faith. He was committed to a great propaganda, to the preaching of Jesus, and he had to preach with penetration and appeal. There they were loyal to the essential idea of Jesus—they were "sons of fact." They read about Jesus, and they knew him, and they knew where they stood. This has been the essence of the Christian religion. Put that alongside of the pitiful defense which Plutarch makes of obscene rites, filthy images, foolish traditions. Who did the thinking in that ancient world? Again and again it was the Christian.

The old religion crumbled and fell, beaten in thought, in morals, in life, in death. And by and by the only name for it was paganism, the religion of the back-country village, of the out-of-the-way places. Christ had conquered. *Dic tropæum passionis, dic triumphalem Crucem,* sang Prudentius—"Sing the trophy of the Passion; sing the all-triumphant Cross." The ancients thought that God repeated the whole history of the universe over and over again, like a cinema show. Some of them thought the kingdoms rise and fall by pure chance. No, said Prudentius, God planned; God developed the history of mankind; he made Rome for his own purposes, for Christ.

What is the explanation of it? We who live in a rational universe, where real results come from real causes, must ask what is the power that has carried the Christian Church to victory over that great old religion. And there is another question: is this story going to be repeated? What is there about Shiva, Kali, or Shri Krishna that essentially differentiates them from the gods of Greece and Rome and Egypt? Tradition, legend, philosophy—point by point, we find the same thing; and we find the same Christian Church, with the same ideals, facing the same conflict. What will be the result? The result will be the same. We have seen in China, in the last two decades, how the Christian Church is true to its traditions; how men can die for Jesus Christ. In the Greek Church—a suffering Church—on the round sacramental wafer there is a cross, and the words "Jesus Christ conquers." That is the story of the Christian Church in the Roman Empire. That is the story which, please God, we shall see again in India. "Jesus Christ conquers."

CHAPTER X

JESUS IN CHRISTIAN THOUGHT

JESUS CHRIST came to men as a great new experience. He took them far outside all they had known of God and of man. He led them, historically, into what was, in truth, a new world, into a new understanding of life in all its relations. What they had never noticed before, he brought to their knowledge, he made interesting to them, and intelligible. In short, as Paul put it, "if any man be in Christ, it is a new creation" (II Cor. v. 17). The aspects of things were different; the values were changed, and a new perspective made clear relations that were obscure and tangled before. Why should it have been so? Why should it be, that, when a man comes into contact, into some kind of sympathy with Jesus Christ, some living union with him, everything becomes new, and he by and by begins to feel with St. Paul: "To me to live is Christ" (Phil. i. 21)? Why has Jesus meant so much? Why should all this be associated with him?

Plato, in the sentence already quoted, tells us that "the unexamined life is unlivable for a human being, for a real man." Here, then, came into man's life a new experience altogether, like nothing known before—altering everything, giving new sympathies, new passions, new enthusiasms—a new attitude to God and a new attitude to men. It was inevitable that thought must work upon it. Who was this Jesus that he should produce this result? Men asked themselves that very early; and if they were slow to do so, the criticism of the outsider drove them into it. The result has been nineteen centuries of endless question and speculation as to Jesus Christ—the rise of dogma, creed, and formula, as slowly all the philosophy of mankind has been re-thought in the light of the central experience of Jesus Christ. In spite of all that we may regret in the war of creeds, it was inevitable—it was part of the disturbance that Jesus foresaw he must make (Luke xii. 51). Men "could do no other"—they had to determine for themselves the significance of Jesus in the real world, in the whole cosmos of God; and it meant fruitful conflict of opinion, the growth of the human mind, and an ever-heightened emphasis on Jesus.

An analogy may illustrate in some way the story before us. One of the most fascinating chapters of geography is the early exploration of America. Chesapeake Bay was missed by one explorer. Fog or darkness may have been the cause of his missing the place; but he missed it, and, though it is undoubtedly there, he made his map without it. Now let us suppose a similar case—for it must often have happened in early days—and this time we will say it was the Hudson, or some river of that magnitude. A later explorer came, and where the map showed a shore without a break, he found a huge inlet or outlet. Was it an arm of the sea, a vast bay, or was it a great river? A very great deal depended on which it was, and the first thing was to determine that. There were several ways of doing it. One was to sail up and map the course. A quicker way was to drop a bucket over the side of the ship. The bucket, we may be sure, went down; and it came up with fresh water; and the water was an instant revelation of several new and important facts. They had discovered, first of all, that where there was an unbroken coast-line on the map, there was nothing of the kind in reality; there was a broad waterway up into the country; and this was not a bay, but the mouth of a river, and a very great river indeed; and this implied yet another discovery—that men had to reckon with no mere island or narrow peninsula, but an immense continent, which it remained to explore.

Jesus Christ was in himself a very great discovery for those to whom he gave himself, and the exploration of him shows a somewhat similar story. Men have often said that they see nothing in him very different from the rest of us; while others have found in him, in the phrase of the Apocalypse (Rev. xxii. 1), the "water of life"; and the positive announcement is here, as in the other case, the more important of the two. The discovery of the volume of life, which comes from Jesus Christ, is one of the greatest that men have made. Merely to have dipped his bucket, as it were, in that great stream of life has again and again meant everything to a man. Think of what the new-found river of the New World meant to some of those early explorers after weeks at sea—

> Water, water everywhere,
> Nor any drop to drink—

and they reach an immense flood of river-water. It was new life at once; but it did not necessarily mean the immediate exploration of everything, the instant completion of geographical discovery. It was life and the promise of more to follow. The history of the Church is a record, we may put it, both of the discovery of the River of Life and of the exploration of its course and its sources, and of what lies behind it. But the discovery and the exploration are different things, and the first is quicker and more certain than the second. Most of us will admit that we have not gone very far up into that Continent. The object of this chapter is not to attempt to survey or compendiarize Christian exploration of Jesus, but to try to find for ourselves a new approach to an estimate of the historical figure who has been and remains the center of everything.

We may classify the records of the Christian exploration roughly in three groups. In the early Christian centuries, we find endless thought given to the philosophical study of the relation of Christ and God. It fills the library of the Early Church, and practically all the early controversies turn upon it. The weak spot in all this was the use of the *a priori* method. Men started with preconceptions about God—not unnaturally, for we all have some theories about God, which we are apt to regard as knowledge. But knowledge is a difficult thing to reach in any sphere of study; and men assumed too quickly that they had attained a sound philosophical account of God. They over-estimated their actual knowledge of God and did not recognize to the full the importance of their new experience. This may seem ungenerous to men, who gave life and everything for Jesus Christ, and to whose devotion, to whose love of Jesus, we owe it that we know him—an ungenerous criticism of their brave thinking, and their independence in a hundred ways of old tradition. Still it is true that the weakness of much of their Christology—and of ours

—is that it starts with a borrowed notion of God, which really has very little to do with the Christian religion. To this we shall return; but in the meantime we may note that here as elsewhere preconceptions have to be lightly held by the serious student. Huxley once wrote to Charles Kingsley: "Science seems to me to teach in the highest and strongest manner the great truth that is embodied in the Christian conception of entire surrender to the will of God. Sit down before the fact as a little child, be prepared to give up every preconceived notion, follow humbly wherever and to whatever end Nature leads, or you shall learn nothing. . . . I have only begun to learn content and peace of mind since I have resolved at all risks to do this." So Huxley wrote about the study of natural science. In this great inquiry of ours we have to learn to be patient enough—we might say, ignorant enough—to do the same. The Early Church had a faith in Greek philosophy, which stood in its way, brave and splendid as its thinkers were.

Our second group is represented roughly by the Hymn Book. The evidential value of a good hymn book will stand investigation. Of course a great many hymns are mere copies, and poor copies; but the Hymn Book at its best is a collection of first-hand records of experience.[1] In the story of the Christian Church doxology comes

[1] Perhaps one may quote here, not inappropriately, the famous saying of Aristotle in his *Poetics*, that "poetry is a more philosophic thing than history, and of a higher seriousness." The latter term means that the poet is "more in earnest" about his work, and puts more energy of mind into it than the historian. If the reader hesitates about this, let him try to write a great hymn or poem.

before dogma. When the writer of the Apocalypse breaks out at the very beginning: "Unto him that loved us and washed[1] us from our sins in his own blood . . . be glory and dominion for ever and ever" (Rev. i. 5), he is recording a great experience; and his doxology leads him on to an explanation of what he has felt and known—to an intellectual judgment and an appreciation of Christ. The order is experience—happiness and song—and then reflection. The love and the cleansing, and the joy, supply the materials on which thought has to work. We have always to remember that thought does not strictly supply its own material, however much it may help us to find it. Philosophy and theology do not give us our facts. Their function is to group and interpret them.

Our third group of records is given to us by the men of the Reformation. We have there two great movements side by side. There is Bible translation, which means, in plain language, a decision or conviction on the part of scholars and thinkers, that the knowledge of the historical Jesus, and of men's first experiences of him, is of the highest importance in the Christian life. The whole Reformation follows, or runs parallel with, that movement. It is essentially a new exploration of what Jesus Christ can do and of what he can be.

In dealing with all these three groups of records, we have to note the seriousness of the men who made the experiments, their energy of mind, their determination to reach real facts and, in Cromwell's great phrase, to "speak things." They will have the truth of the matter.

[1] Do not let us be misled by the thin pedantries of the Revised Version here, or in Romans v. 1 shortly to be cited. In both places literary and spiritual sense has bowed to the accidents of MSS.

Intricate and entangled as is the history, for instance, of the Arian controversy—that controversy which "turned on a diphthong," as Carlyle said in his younger days—it represented far more than mere logomachy, as Carlyle saw later on. It followed from a determination to get at the real fact of who and what Jesus Christ is; and the two words, that differed by a diphthong, embodied diametrically opposite conceptions of him. With all the supersubtlety that sometimes characterizes theologians, these men had a passion for truth. It led them into paths where our minds find a difficulty in following; but the motive was the imperative sense that thinking men must examine and understand their supreme experience—a motive that must weigh with men who are in earnest about life.

The great hymns of the Church—such as the *Dies Iræ* of Thomas of Celano, or Bernard's *Jesu dulcis memoria*, or Toplady's *Rock of Ages*—are transcripts from life, made by deep-going and serious minds. The writers are recording, with deep conviction of its worth, what they have discovered in experience. A man who takes Christ seriously and will "examine life," will often find in those great hymns, it may be with some surprise, an anticipation of his own experience—as Bunyan did in Luther's Commentary on *Galatians*. Livingstone had *Jesu dulcis memoria*—the Latin of it—ringing in his head as he traveled in unexplored Africa. Men who did such work —work that lasts and is recognized again and again to be genuine by others busy in the same field—cannot have been random, light-hearted creatures. They were, in fact, men tested in life, men of experience—of wide and deep experience—men with a gift for living, developed in heart as well as in brain. The finest of Greek critics, Longinus, said that, "The great style (*hupsos*) is an echo of a great soul." Neander said—and it is again and again true—that "it is the heart that makes the theologian." Where we find a great hymn or a great theology, we may be sure of finding a great nature and a great experience behind it.

Let us sum up our general results so far. First of all, whatever be the worth of the consensus of Christian opinion—and we have to decide how much it is worth, bearing in mind the type of man who has worked and suffered to make it in every age; and, I think, it runs high, as the work of serious and explorative minds—the consensus of Christian opinion gives the very highest name to Jesus Christ. Men, who did not begin with any preconception in his favor, and who have often had a great deal of difficulty in explaining to others—and perhaps to themselves—the course by which they have reached their conclusions, claim the utmost for Jesus—and this in spite of the most desperate philosophical difficulties about monotheism. With a strong sense of fact, with a deepening feeling for reality, with a growing value for experience, and with bolder ventures upon experience, men have found that their conception of Jesus deepens and grows; he means more to them the more they are. And, as was noted in the first chapter, in a rational universe, where truth counts and error fails, the Church has risen in power with every real emphasis laid on Jesus Christ. What does this involve?

So far our records. To-day we are living in an era when great scientific discoveries are made, and more are promised. Geology once unsettled people about *Genesis*; but closer study of the Bible and of science has given truer views of both, and thinking people are as little troubled about geology now as about Copernican astronomy. At present heredity and psychology are dominating our minds—or, rather, theories as to both; for though beginnings have been made, the stage has not yet been reached of very wide or certain discovery. There is still a great deal of the soul unexplored and unmapped. No reasonable person would wish to belittle the study either of evolution or of psychology; but the real men of science would probably urge that lay people should take more pains to know the exact meaning and scope of scientific terms, and to have some more or less clear idea in their minds when they use them. However, all these modern discoveries and theories are, to many men's minds, a challenge to the right of Christians to speak of Jesus Christ as they have spoken of him, a challenge to our right to represent the facts of Christian life as we have represented them—in other words, they are a challenge to us to return to experience and to see what we really mean. If our study of Jesus in the preceding chapters has been on sound lines, we shall feel that the challenge to face facts is in his vein; it was what he urged upon men throughout.

The old problem returns upon us: Who and what is this Jesus Christ? We are involved in the recurrent need to re-examine him and re-explore him.

There are several ways of doing so. Like every other historical character Jesus is to be known by what he does rather than by *a priori* speculation as to what he might be. In the study of history the first thing is to know our original documents. There are the Gospels, and, like other historical records, they must be studied in earnest on scientific lines without preconception. And there are later records, which tell us as plainly and as truthfully of what he has done in the world's history. We can begin, then, with the serious study of the actual historical Jesus, whom people met in the road and with whom they ate their meals, whom the soldiers nailed to the cross, whom his disciples took to worshiping, and who has, historically, re-created the world.

The second line of approach is rather more difficult, but with care we can use Christological theories to recover the facts which those who framed the theories intended to explain. We must remember here once more the three historical canons laid down at the beginning. We must above all things give the man's term his meaning, and ask what was the experience behind his thought. When we come upon such descriptions of Jesus as "Christ our Passover" (1 Cor. v. 7), or find him called the Messiah, we must not let our own preconceptions as to the value of the theories implied by the use of such language, nor again our existing views of what is orthodox, determine our conclusions; but we must ask what those who so explained Jesus really meant to say, and what they had experienced which they thought worth expressing. These people, as we see, were face to face with a very great new experience, and they cast about for some means of describing and explaining it. A slight illustration may suggest the natural law in accordance with which they set about their task of explanation. A child, of between two and three years old, was watching his first snow-storm, gazing very intently at the flying snow-flakes, and evidently trying to think out what they were. At last he hit it; they were "little birds."

It is so that the mind, infant or adult, is apt to work—explaining the new and unknown by reference to the familiar. Snow-flakes are not little birds; they are something quite different; yet there is a common element—they both go flying through the air, and it was that fact which the child's brain noticed and used. To explain Jesus, his friends and contemporaries spoke of him as the Logos, the Sacrifice, "Christ our Passover," the Messiah, and so forth. Of those terms not one is intelligible to us to-day without a commentary. To ordinary people Jesus is at once intelligible—far more so than the explanations of him. Historically, it is he himself who has antiquated every one of those conceptions, and, so far as they have survived, it has been in virtue of association with him. They are the familiar language of another day. "No one," said Dr. Rendel Harris, "can sing, 'How sweet the name of Logos sounds.'" Synesius of Cyrene did try to sing it, but most human beings prefer St. Bernard or John Newton.

The inner significance of each term will point to the real experience of the man using it. He employs a metaphor, a simile, or a technical term to explain something. Can we penetrate to the analogy which he finds between the Jesus of the new experience and the old term which he uses? Can we, when we see what he has experienced, grasp the substance and build on that to the neglect of the term? When we look at the terms, we find that the essence of sacrifice was reconciliation between God and man (we shall return to this a little later), and that the Messiah was understood to be destined to achieve God's purpose and God's meaning for mankind and for each man. We find, again, that the inner meaning of the Logos is that through it, and in it, God and man come in touch with each other and become mutually intelligible. Reconciliation, the victory of God, the mutual intelligibility of God and man—all three terms center in one great thought, a new union between God and man. That, so far as I can see, is the common element; and that is, as men have conceived it, the very heart of the Christian experience.

In the third place, we can utilize the new experiments made upon Jesus Christ in the Reformation and in other revivals. They come nearer to us; for the men who report are more practical and more scholarly in the modern way; they are more akin to us both in blood and in ideas. Luther, for example, is a great spirit of the explorer type. He went to scholarship and learnt the true meaning of *metanoia*—that it was "re-thinking" and not "penance"—and he grasped a new view of God there. From scholarship he gained a truer view of Church history than he had been taught; and this too helped to clear his mind. Above all, as "a great son of fact" (Carlyle's name for him), his chief interest was the exploration of Jesus Christ—would Christ stand all the weight that a man could throw upon him without assistance? And Luther found that Christ could; and he at once turned his knowledge into action, as the world knows. "Justification by faith" was his phrase, and he meant that we may trust Jesus Christ with all that we are, all that we have been, and all that we hope to be; that Jesus himself will carry all; that Jesus himself *is* all; that Jesus is at once Luther's eternal salvation, and his sure help in the next day's difficulty—his Saviour for ever from sin, and his great stand-by in translating the Bible for the German people and in writing hymns for boys and girls.[1] *Nos nihil sumus*, he wrote, *Christus solus est omnia.* In the case of every great revival—the Wesleyan revival, and the smaller ones in the United States, in the north of Ireland, in Wales—in every one we find that, where anything is really achieved, it is done by a new and thoroughgoing emphasis on Jesus Christ. It may be put in language which to some ears is repulsive, in metaphors strange or uncouth; but whatever the language, the fact that underlies it is this—men are brought back to the reality, the presence, the power, and the friendship of Jesus Christ; they are called to a fresh venture on Jesus Christ, a fresh exploration: and again and again the experience of a lifetime has justified the venture.

This brings us to the most effective and fundamental method in the exploration of Jesus, in some ways the most difficult of all, or else the very simplest. The Church has been clear that there is nothing like personal experiment, the personal venture. It is the only clue to the experience. The saying of one of the old Latin fathers, *Credo ut intelligam*, is to many of our minds offensive—I think, because we give the wrong meaning to his *Credo.* But, if the illustrations are not too simple, swimming and bicycling offer parallels. A man will never understand how water holds up a human body, as long as he stays on dry land. In practical things, the venture comes first; and it is hard to see how a man is to understand Christ without a personal experience of him. All parents know how much better bachelors and maiden sisters understand children than they do; but as soon as these great authori-

[1] If my readers do not know his Christmas hymn for children, they have missed one of the happiest hymns for Christmas.

ties have children of their own, the position is altered a little.

The change that Jesus definitely operates in men, they have described in various ways—rebirth, salvation, a new heart, and so forth. What they have always emphasized in Jesus Christ, is that they find he changes their outlook and develops new instincts in them, and that in one way and another he saves from sin; and they have been men who have learnt and adopted Jesus' own estimate of sin. When, then, we remember that, with his serious view of sin, he undertook man's redemption from it; when we add to this some real reflection upon how much he has already done, as plain matter of history, to "take away the sin of the world," we surely have something to go upon in our attempt to determine who he is. The question will rise, Have Christians overstated their experience, or even misunderstood it? Has forgiveness been, in fact, achieved—or salvation from sin? Can sin be put away at all? What will the evidence for this be? I do not know what the evidence could be, except the new life of peace with God, and all the sunshine and blessing that go with it. This new life is at all events all the evidence available; and how much it means is very difficult to estimate without some personal experience.

Here again the great theories of Redemption will help us to recover the experience they are to explain; and once more we may note that they are not the work of small minds or trivial natures, however badly they have been echoed. Substitution implies at any rate some serious confession of guilt before God, some strong sense of a great indebtedness to Christ. The theory of Sacrifice implies the need of reunion with God. Robertson Smith, in his "Early Religion of the Semites," brings out that the essence of ancient sacrifice was that the tribe, the sacrificial beast and the god were all of one blood; the god was supposed to be alienated; the sacrifice was offered by the party to the quarrel who was seeking reconciliation, namely, the tribe. When we look at the New Testament, we find that the emphasis always lies on God seeking reconciliation with man (*cf.* 2 Cor. v. 19). The theory of ransom—a most moving term in a world of slavery—implies the need of new freedom for the mind, for the heart and the whole nature, from the tyranny of sin. All these are similes; and tremendous structures of theory have been built on every one of them—and for some of these structures, simile, or, in plainer language, analogy, is not a sufficient foundation. It is probably true that all our current explanations of the work of Christ in Redemption have in them too large an element of metaphor and simile. Yet Christian people are reluctant to discard any one of them; and their reluctance is intelligible. There is a value in the old association, which is found by new experience. Every one of these old similes will contribute to our realization of the work of Christ, in so far as it is a record of experience of Christ, verified in one generation after another. We shall make the best use of them, when we are no longer intimidated by the terminology, but go at once to what is meant—to the facts.

We come still closer to the facts in the less metaphorical terms of the New Testament. For example, there is the New Covenant. The writer of the Epistle to the Hebrews went back to a great phrase in Jeremiah, and by his emphasis on it he helped to give its name to the whole New Testament—"I will make a new covenant with the house of Israel and the house of Judah" (Heb. viii. 8-12; Jer. xxxi. 31-34). Using this passage, he brings out that there is a new relation, a new union, between God and man in Jesus. He speaks of Jesus as a mediator bringing man and God together (Heb. viii. 6)—language far plainer to us than the terminology of sacrifice, which he employed rather to bring home the work of Jesus with feeling and passion to those who had no other vocabulary, than to impose upon Christian thinkers a scheme of things which he clearly saw to be exhausted. Then there is Paul's great conception of Reconciliation (2 Cor. v. 18-20). Half the difficulties connected with the word "Atonement" disappear, when we grasp that the word in Greek means primarily reconciliation. As Paul uses the noun and the verb, it is very plain what he means—God is in Christ trying to reconcile the world to himself. These attempts to express Christ's work in plain words take us back to the great central Christian experience—to the great initial discovery that the discord of man's making between God and man has been removed by God's overtures in Christ; that the obstacles which man has felt to his approach to God—in the unclean hands and the unclean lips—have been taken away; and that with a heart, such as the human heart is, a man may yet come to God in Jesus, because of Jesus, through Jesus.

The historical character of Christian life and thought is surely evidence that Jesus Christ has accomplished something real; and when we get a better hold of that, the problem of his person should be more within our reach. The splendid phrase of Paul—"Therefore being justified by faith, we have peace with God through our Lord Jesus Christ" (Rom. v. 1)—or that of 1 Peter: "In whom ye rejoice . . . with joy unspeakable and full of glory" (1 Pet. i. 8)—gives us the keynote. The gaiety of the Early Church in its union with Jesus Christ rings through the New Testament and the Christian fathers from Hermas to Augustine. The Church has come singing down the ages.[1] The victory over sin—no easy thing at any time—is another permanent feature of Christian experience. The psychological value of what Dr. Chalmers called "the expulsive power of a new affection" is not enough studied by us. Look at the freedom, the growth, the power of the Christian life—where do they all come from? We cannot leave God out of this. At any rate, there they are in the Christian experience; and where does anything that matters flow from but from God? There is again the evidence of Christian achievement; and it should be remarked that the Christian always tells us that he himself has not the power, that it comes from God, that he asks for it and God gives it. As for the easy explanation of all religious life by "auto-suggestion," we may note that it involves a loose and unscientific use of a more or less scientific theory —never a very safe way to knowledge. In any case, it has been pointed out, the word adds nothing to the number of our facts; nor is it quite clear yet that it eliminates God from the story any more than the term "digestion" makes it inappropriate to say Grace before meat. All these things—peace, joy, victory, and the rest—follow from the taking away of sin, and imply that it no longer stands between God and man. All this is the work of the historical Jesus. It is he who has changed the attitude of

[1] What Carlyle says in "The Hero as a Poet" (*Heroes and Hero Worship*) on the close relation of Song and Truth is worth remembering in this connection.

man to God, and by changing it has made it possible for God to do what he has done. If God, in Paul's phrase, "hath shined in our hearts" (2 Cor. iv. 6), it was Jesus who induced men to take down the shutters and to open the windows. It is all associated, historically, with the ever-living Jesus Christ, and with God in him.

This brings us to the central question, the relation of Jesus with God—the problem of Incarnation. After all that has been said, we shall not approach it *a priori*. We are too apt to put the Incarnation more or less in algebraic form:

$$x + y = a,$$

where a stands for the historical Jesus Christ, and x and y respectively for God and man. But what do we mean by x and y? Let us face our facts. What do we know of man apart from Jesus Christ? Surely it is only in him that we realize man—only in him that we grasp what human depravity really is, the real meaning and implications of human sin. It is those who have lived with Jesus Christ, who are most conscious of sin; and this is no mere morbid imagination or fancy, it rests on a much deeper exploration of human nature than men in general attempt. Not until we know what he is do we see how very little we are, and how far we have gone wrong. It is his power of help and sympathy that teaches us the hardness of our own hearts, our own fundamental want of sympathy. Again, until a man knows Jesus Christ, he has little chance of even guessing the grandeur of which he himself is capable. A man has, as he says, done his best—for years, it may be, of strenuous endeavor; and then comes the new experience of Jesus Christ, and he is lifted high above his record, he gains a new power, a new tenderness, and he does things incredible. We do not know the wrong or the right of which man is capable, till we know Jesus Christ. The y of our equation, then, does not tell us very much.

When it comes to the x, is it not very often a mixture —an ill-adjusted mixture—of the Father of Jesus, with the rather negative "beyond all being" of later Greek speculation, and perhaps the Judge of Roman law? The exact proportions in the mixture will vary with the thinker. But, in fact, is it not true now that we really only know God through Jesus? For it is only in and through Jesus that we take the trouble, and have the faith, to explore and test God, to try experiments upon God, to know what he can do and what he will do. It is only in Jesus that the Love of God, in the New Testament sense, is tenable at all. It is evanescent apart from Jesus; it rests on the assurance of his words, his work, his personality. A vague diffused "love of God" for everything in general and nothing in particular, we saw to be a quite different thing from the personal attachment, with which, according to Jesus, God loves the individual man. That is the center of the Gospel; it is belief in that, which has done everything in a rational world, as we saw at the beginning; and it is a most impossible belief, never long or very actively held apart from Jesus. Only in him can we believe it. Only in him, too, is the new experience of God's forgiveness and redemption possible, in all its fulness and sureness and power. "*Dieu me pardonnera,*" said Heine, "*c'est son métier*"; but he had not the Christian sense of what it was that God was to forgive. It is only in Jesus that we can live the real life of prayer, in the intimate way of Jesus. All this means that we have to solve our x from Jesus—not to discover him through it. The plain fact is that we actually know Jesus a great deal better than we know our x and our y, the elements from which we hoped to reconstruct him. What does this mean?

It means, bluntly, that we have to re-think our theories of Incarnation on *a posteriori* lines, to begin on facts that we know, and to base ourselves on a continuous exploration and experience of Jesus Christ first. The simple, homely rule of knowing things before we talk about them holds in every other sphere of study, and it is the rule which Jesus himself inculcated. We begin, then, with Jesus Christ, and set out to see how far he will take us. Experience comes first. "Follow me," he said. He chose the twelve men "that they might be with him," and he let them find out in that intercourse what he had for them; and from what he could give and did give they drew their conclusions as to who and what he is. There can be no other way of knowing him. "Luther's Reformation doctrines," says Hermann, in his fine book, *The Union of the Christian with God* (p. 163), "only countenance such a confession of the Deity of Christ as springs naturally to the lips of the man whom Jesus has already made blessed." Melanchthon said the same: "This it is to know Christ—to receive his benefits—not to contemplate his natures, or the modes of his incarnation." "Come unto me, all ye that labor and are heavy laden, and I will give you rest."